Black Film Stars

Black Film Stars

by EILEEN LANDAY

DRAKE PUBLISHERS INC.
NEW YORK

Published in 1973 by
Drake Publishers Inc.
381 Park Avenue South
New York, N.Y. 10016

Library of Congress Cataloging in Publication Data
Landay, Eileen
Black film stars
1. Negro moving-picture actors and actresses.
I. Title.
PN1998.A2L33.   791.43'028'0922   73-5564
ISBN 0-87749-508-4

Printed in the United States of America

Prepared and produced for the publisher by BMG
Productions, Incorporated

THIS BOOK IS FOR THE LEARNING TREE

To the librarians and pages at the Lincoln Center Library of the Performing Arts, and especially to Monty Arnold.

To Stephen Harvey, Charles Silvers, and Mary Corliss of the Museum of Modern Art Film Study Center.

To the librarians at the Schomberg Collection, New York Public Library.

To the librarians at the Westbury Memorial Public Library and especially to Pat Gleason and Marion Brescia.

And to Andy Clifford, Jamie Clifford, and Karen Frishkoff, Bruce Frishkoff, Ben Clinesmith, and Kathleen Clinesmith.

Thank you.

CREDITS

Brown Brothers — Pages: 22, 24, 25 (top).

Cinemabilia — Pages: 162, 164 (bottom right), 167 (upper left), 176, 179, 180, 181, 182.

Culver Pictures, Inc. — Pages: 17, 18, 19 (top and bottom), 23, 25 (bottom), 29, 41, 51, 52, 55, 78, 80 (top), 87 (right).

Lincoln Center Library of the Performing Arts (Photographed by Meryl Joseph) — Pages: 49, 54 (top), 60, 61 (bottom), 73 (left), 80 (bottom), 86 (right) 87 (left), 93, 94, 95 (bottom), 112, 131, 135, 138, 145, 153, 155, 164 (left), 165, 167 (upper right), 174.

Memory Shop — Pages: 36, 67 (right), 86 (left), 88, 89, 91, 117, 119, 120, 124 (top), 125, 128, 130 (right), 134, 136, 137, 140 (bottom), 144 (left), 150 (right), 159, 168, 173, 175, 184, 185, 186, 187, 189.

The Museum of Modern Art/Film Stills Archive—Pages: 26, 27, 31, 32, 33 (top and bottom) 34, 37, 38, 39, 40, 42, 43, 44, 46, 50, 54, (bottom), 56, 57, 58, 59, 61 (top), 62, 64, 65, 66, 67 (left), 68, 69, 70, 71, 72, 73 (right), 74, 75, 76, 77, 79, 83, 84, 85, 90, 92, 95 (top), 97, 98, 99, 101, 104, 105, 106, 107, 108, 109, 110, 111, 113, 114, 115, 118, 121, 122, 123, 124 (bottom), 127, 129, 130 (left-top and bottom), 132, 133, 139, 140 (top), 141, 142, 143, 144 (right), 146, 147, 148, 150 (left), 151, 154, 157, 158, 160, 161, 163, 164 (top right), 167 (bottom, left and right), 169, 170, 171, 172, 177, 178, 183, 188.
Schomburg Center for Research in Black Culture, the New York Public Library — Page: 45.

Wide World Photos, Inc. — Page 152.

Quotations from "Nobody" by Bert Williams, page 23, and "Brown Baby" by Oscar Brown, Jr., page 134, © copyright Edward B. Marks Music Corporation. Used by permission.

Quotation on page 93, by permission of the author, Mari Evans, from *I Am A Black Woman*, published by William Morrow & Co., 1970.

Contents

In April 1896, Thomas Edison's moving pictures were first shown to an astounded audience at Koster and Bial's Music Hall in New York City. In the same year, the U.S. Supreme Court upheld the conviction of Mr. Homer Plessy, a black man, for sitting down in a "white" car on a Louisiana railroad train.

Powered by newly harnessed electricity and the steam engine, the nineteenth century was speeding to a close. Over the course of the century, in apparent dizzying succession, the railroad, steamship, telegraph, telephone, phonograph, and internal combustion engine had appeared. Now would come what Frederick Lewis Allen called "the big change," the industrialization of most of a nation in a period of fifty years. There were then nine million blacks in the United States, most of them living in the rural South and just half a century away from slavery.

During the seventy years to come, Mr. Edison's "flickers" were to have a profound effect on all Americans—black and white, audience and performers. This story is an attempt to trace the path of the black in movies, marking the milestones, tragedies, ironies, and humor of the journey. It is a memorial to Bert Williams, genius glimmering through blackface; to the integrity of Charles Gilpin; to the unexplored talents of Nina Mae McKinney, Daniel Haynes, Fredi Washington, and a thousand brothers and sisters; to the determination and little-known achievements of Oscar Micheaux; to the humanity and stature of Paul Robeson, a man ahead of his times; to the talents of Stepin Fetchit, Bill Robinson, Butterfly McQueen, and Hattie McDaniel that rose above the consciousness of the years in which they worked; to the beauty and tragedy of Dorothy Dandridge; to the dignity of Ethel Waters; and to all the others who came before Sidney Poitier.

It is the story of those who followed Poitier and their places in the journey. It is a social history, a diary, a study in human behavior, a lesson in economics, a counterpoint of talent wasted and talent triumphant—one which might lead us to wonder if we have reached the journey's end or have taken only the first few halting steps along the way. It begins in 1896.

With Mr. Plessy's conviction, Jim Crow became the law of the land. Only one Supreme Court justice had opposed the decision. In his dissenting opinion, Justice John Marshall Harlan wrote, "there is in this country no superior dominant ruling class of citizens. There is no caste here. Our Constitution is color-blind . . . ." None of his fellow justices agreed.

Blacks were despised, powerless, and poor. At a time when Andrew Carnegie's annual income exceeded twenty-five million dollars, most blacks earned less than seventy-five cents a day. Almost half of them could not read or write. Most were sharecroppers or tenant farmers who found themselves, each year, deeper and deeper in debt to the farm owner and tied closer to their servitude.

Although the black male's right to vote was guaranteed by the Fifteenth Amendment in 1870, he was forced to meet complex property and literacy requirements and pay a poll tax as well—measures so effective that in 1900 in Alabama, only 3,000 out of 180,000 eligible black men were able to vote.

Southern states and towns were in the process of writing a paralyzing web of laws and ordinances, so that each time a black left his home, he had to brace himself to meet degrading problems arising from his Jim Crow status. Waiting rooms, ticket windows, water fountains, trains, trolleys, boarding houses—all had signs designating: WHITES ONLY or COLORED.

A South Carolina law prohibited textile workers of different races from using the same doorways, stairs, or pay windows. In Mobile, a curfew applying to blacks only required them to be off the streets by 10:00 P.M. Ten states required total segregation in jails and prisons. Almost all southern hospitals were segregated and many refused to treat blacks at all.

In Virginia and North Carolina, any club or society in which members of different races called each other "brother" was illegal. A Louisiana law dealing with circuses and sideshows specified that exits, entrances, and ticket windows be separated by at least twenty-five feet. An Atlanta ordinance required each courtroom to have two Bibles: one for swearing in white witnesses, and a Jim Crow Bible for swearing in black witnesses.

In actual fact, the black in the South had not one human right a white had to respect—including even the right to life. In the year 1901, 130 lynchings were recorded; in many southern communities, such gang murders had become an accepted social institution.

Throughout the nation, the "big change" was going on. The night the audience at Koster and Bial's first saw pictures move, they clapped and screamed their excitement. Soon the "flickers" had star billing in vaudeville houses all over the country. Audiences rushed to darkened theatres to watch pictures of waves crashing over rocks or the Pennsylvania Limited thundering toward them at sixty miles an hour.

But these same audiences tired of the novelty and soon the "galloping tintypes" were relegated to the rear of penny arcades and to dark, damp, and dirty "store shows"—places considered repulsive by respectable people. The "poor man's show" appealed to the lowest classes. It was not necessary to read or write to understand the movies with their appeal to the senses or simple, exaggerated movements. And the admission—only a nickel—allowed all but the destitute to attend.

As the nickels of the poor began to pour into their hands, penny arcade owners and a horde of other show business hangers-on saw the "flickers" as a way to get rich. They converted the penny arcades and empty stores into "nickelodeons." The demand grew and films improved.

"One reelers" were shot in studios such as Thomas Edison's Black Maria in New Jersey or outdoors at beaches, parks, or on city streets. The bulky cameras were set up, and as the cameraman cranked away, the "story" that passed before it was recorded on film.

Tom Fletcher, a well-known black minstrel, gave one of the earliest descriptions of the black in films in his autobiography: "My partner Al Barley and I got leading comedy parts. The studio was on 22nd Street between Broadway and Fourth Avenue. I was the talent scout for the colored people. There were no types, just colored men, women and children. There were no script writers, no make-up artists, wardrobe mistresses. . . . There was just one man. Everybody called him Mr. Porter and I never took the time to find out his first name. He placed you in your position and gave you your actions, lit the scene and turned the camera. At the end of each day, I got eight dollars.

We all considered it a lot of fun with pay."

Little record remains of those earliest days of filmmaking in which blacks appeared. As it changed from "fun with pay" to more serious business, blacks were no longer hired. Instead, their roles were played by whites wearing burnt cork and wooly wigs, a custom which continued almost without exception until after World War I. Whatever other reasons there may have been, blacks were judged too ignorant to play themselves on the screen.

In 1904 Biograph Film Studios produced *A Bucket of Cream Ale,* a short film in which a white customer angrily shouts at a black waitress for taking a sip from his pitcher. She watches, listens, then pours the contents over his head. The film is over and with it a brief, almost forgotten victory. In no other movie for the next forty years was the black given a chance to fight back. *The Wooing and Wedding of a Coon* (1905) was more typical. Billed as a "genuine Ethiopian comedy," the film described "the antics of two shiftless, head-scratching darkies." This portrayal of black man as fool continued in the later roles of Mantan Moreland, Willie Best, and Stepin Fetchit.

Another stereotype, that of the black as vicious brute, was introduced first in *Fights of Nations* (1905). In it, the black was described as a "razor thrower," the Mexican as "treacherous," the Jew as a "briber," the Spaniard as a "foppish lover," and the Irishman as a "drunkard." In the final scene, the white American, the "bearer of peace," triumphs gloriously. This movie aptly portrayed the imperialist mood of the times. Having fought and won the Spanish-American war, the United States had taken up the white man's burden, the "divine right of the Caucasian to govern."

Yet when Teddy Roosevelt's Rough Riders climbed San Juan Hill, black troops of the Ninth and Tenth Cavalries accompanied them. After the battle, Roosevelt said, "Well, the Ninth and Tenth men are all right! They can drink out of our canteens." As if to prove his point, Roosevelt invited Booker T. Washington to dinner at the White House shortly after becoming president. Black leaders had attended meetings at the White House before, but dinner was a different matter. Southern whites were outraged, and news articles and editorials reflected their fury. Although Roosevelt made no public reply, he privately admitted that he had "gone too far."

If any black person should have been considered "fit" to dine with the president, it was Booker T. Washington. The determined ex-slave, founder and president of Tuskeegee Institute and acknowledged leader of blacks in America, had always preached moderation to members of his race. He reminded them "that to seek social equality is the extremest folly." The purpose of his institute, as he explained, was to create first-rate mechanical laborers who would serve the South. Money poured into Tuskegee from northern philanthropists. The *New York World* called Washington the "Negro Moses." Even the South tolerated him.

In opposition to Washington's willingness to pacify whites, a group of twenty-nine black leaders gathered in 1905 to form the Niagara Movement. They met on the Canadian side of the border after hotels on the American side had refused to house them. Their spokesman was W. E. B. DuBois, a quiet, formal young professor, the first black to earn a Ph.D. at Harvard, who had a passionate interest in equal rights for blacks. He declared, "We claim for ourselves every right that belongs to a free-born American, civil and social, and until we get these rights, we shall never cease to protest and assail the ears of America with the stories of its shameful deeds toward us."

Meanwhile, the movie studios gave the nation films such as *The Masher* (1907), in which a pathetically unsuccessful ladies' man approaches a veiled lady. He lifts her veil, discovers she is black, and is so horrified he runs away, presumably cured of his vice by shock treatment.

A similar story was dramatized in *The Dark Romance of a Tobacco Can* (1911), in which a man who needs a wife in order to collect an inheritance proposes by mail to a woman whose name he finds in a tobacco can. No inheritance can calm the terror he feels when he discovers the woman is colored.

Equally characteristic of the motion-picture image were two series produced around 1910, the *Rastus* and *Sambo* films, which chronicled the odd adventures of an eye-rolling black clown. And *Coon Town Suffragettes* (1910) took a long laugh at a group of colored washerwomen who organized an attempt to keep their worthless husbands out of saloons. Evidence of how standard the image had become is found in a book titled *How to Write Motion Picture Plays*, published in 1913, which describes the following sample plot in a section called "How to Write

Comedy": "A shiftless, worthless fat Negro finds a rabbit's foot which brings him an abundance of melon, pork chops, fried chicken and other things dear to a darky's heart."

Although the early days of film were generally notable for their slapstick, stereotyped characters, and exaggerated actions, the treatment of the black was unique in the fact that he was degraded consistently and *almost without exception.*

In 1908, following bloody race riots just blocks from Abraham Lincoln's home in Springfield, Illinois, a group of distinguished white leaders announced plans to form the National Association for the Advancement of Colored People (NAACP). Members of the Niagara Movement joined them. In their magazine, *Crisis,* editor DuBois wrote: "We have crawled and pleaded for justice and we have been cheerfully spit upon and murdered and burned. We will not endure it forever. If we are to die, in God's name, let us perish like men and not like bales of hay."

Uncle Tom's Cabin

Edwin S. Porter produced the first film version of *Uncle Tom's Cabin* in 1903. In the years that followed, there have been at least six others.

The first was twelve minutes long, fourteen scenes with a descriptive title between each. This film was the earliest on record in which titles were used and the most elaborate effort at telling a story in moving pictures to that date. The feature players were white; blacks found parts among the extras. A Lubin production was released in 1909, and a Vitagraph production in 1910. In 1913, the Universal version in four reels starred Harry Pollard as Uncle Tom.

The Peerless production in 1914 starred Sam Lucas, veteran black vaudevillian, as Uncle Tom, and to Lucas should probably go the official title—"first black star." Though the movie was successful, it was a personal tragedy for him, according to Tom Fletcher's report in his autobiography. After the scene in which Uncle

The 1913 Universal production with Harry Pollard (left) as Uncle Tom, Robert Z. Leonard as Simon Legree (center), and Edna Mason as Eliza.

Tom jumps in the icy river to save Little Eva, Lucas caught cold, developed a lingering illness and finally died. The interesting thing about the 1918 Paramount version was the performance of white actress Marguerite Clark, who played Topsy in blackface as well as Little Eva.

In 1927 Universal was slated to film *Uncle Tom's Cabin* for the second time, and Harry Pollard, the blackface Uncle Tom of 1913, was to be the director. He hired Charles Gilpin, the exciting black actor who had been starring in *The Emperor Jones* at the Provincetown Playhouse, to play Uncle Tom. Gilpin went to Hollywood, reportedly for a salary of $1,000 a week, began rehearsals, and immediately clashed with Pollard over the interpretation of the role. He refused to play the part and, returning to New York, took a job operating an elevator. He later retired to a chicken farm in New Jersey and died shortly thereafter.

Gilpin was replaced in the film by James B. Lowe. His protests may have had some effect, however, because as a reviewer later wrote, the 1927 Uncle Tom "wore his ball and chain in a different way." Topsy was played by Mona Ray in blackface and the white villain, Simon Legree, by George Siegmann, who had once been Silas Lynch, the blackface villain of *The Birth of a Nation*. In 1958 Universal attempted to re-release the same production with an added prologue and sound track featuring Raymond Massey as Abe Lincoln. Civil rights groups protested and the film's run was brief.

In all of the film versions the indictment of slavery, the central theme of Harriet Beecher Stowe's novel, was subtly distorted. Uncle Tom's principle characteristic—submission with a smile—was elevated to a virtue.

Above: Eliza (Marguerita Fischer) is separated from her child (Lassie Lou Ahern) in the 1927 Universal production.   Below: "Little Eva's spirits touched the life of Uncle Tom like a sunbeam in a darkened room." Virginia Grey is little Eva.

Uncle Tom's Cabin was followed by films such as *For Massa's Sake,* in which a "true and faithful slave" tries to sell himself and his family to pay off his master's gambling debt. *The Debt* (1912), The *Octoroon* (1913), and *In Slavery Days* (1913) are all built around "the tragedy of mixed blood." In all three films, the message is the same: "white" blood is good; "black" blood is bad; and "mixed" blood is a disaster.

Historians have called the period which began in 1912 the "Progressive" era. Crusaders such as Teddy Roosevelt and Robert M. LaFollette founded national Progressive parties—Roosevelt in 1912, and LaFollette in 1924; journalists published flaming indictments of poverty and political corruption; the Rockefeller and Carnegie foundations were just being formed. Reformers had begun to press for workman's compensation, labor rights, pure food and drug laws, consumer protection, woman's rights and election reform.

But little had changed for blacks. In 1912, southern-born-and-reared Woodrow Wilson was elected, promising "New Freedoms" for all. But as Paul Robeson later described him, "Wilson was an advocate of democracy for the world and Jim Crow for America." Shortly after his election, he issued an executive order segregating black and white clerks in federal offices. Partitions were erected and the races separated. Wilson told a black committee of inquiry: "Segregation is not humiliating, but a benefit, and ought to be so regarded by you gentlemen."

In 1914 a labor depression drove wages down below seventy cents a day. The boll weevil destroyed most of the cotton crop and summer floods left thousands homeless.

Whenever life grew unbearable to the southern black, he thought about "following the drinking gourd"—the Big Dipper, which pointed to the North and freedom. In years past, it had been freedom from slavery; after Emancipation, it was freedom from starvation and the oppression of Jim Crow. They poured northward into the cities—sons and daughter of slaves, no longer tied to the old way of life—running from a world of sharecropping and lynching parties.

In the three years between 1915 and 1918, nearly a million blacks moved to the North. There they found jobs, but they were bottom-of-the-barrel jobs. Living conditions were poor. The mortality rate was high. Many died from colds, pneumonia, and consumption, proving to anyone who wanted to believe it that "people of the colored race cannot survive in cold climates."

Southern whites migrated north, too, and brought their racial feelings with them. Harlem, Detroit, Chicago, Pittsburgh—blacks soon discovered that none were the "promised land."

Bert Williams

At first the stage was dark. Then a small spotlight came up on a tall, shambling man wearing a patched and ragged suit. Clearly he was a victim of bad luck and a world too hard to understand. Slowly, the man raised his head and tipped it to one side. His eyes opened wider. Without knowing why, the audience began to chuckle, then laugh, then howl, then clap as Bert Williams began to sing his theme song.

Bert Williams and George Walker in 1897

When life seems full of clouds and rain
And I am full of nothin' but pain
Who soothes my thumpin',
    bumpin' brain?
Nobody!
I ain't never done nothin' to nobody
I ain't never got nothin' from nobody,
    no time
Until I get somethin' from somebody,
    some time
I'll never do nothin' for nobody,
    no time

Bert Williams was the first black to win the whole-hearted admiration of theatre audiences and the first to appear regularly on the Broadway stage; the first black recording star and the first to appear in command performance before the King of England. His salary at the height of his fame equaled that of the president of the United States. A *Variety* poll taken twenty-five years after his death in 1927 chose him as one of the ten most important comedians in the history of the American theatre. Eddie Cantor, Red Skelton, Al Jolson, Amos 'n Andy—all learned their art by watching and studying the world of Bert Williams.

There is no doubt that he was a star. To call him a movie star requires a great stretch of the imagination. But he did make movies. And his life so perfectly describes the dilemma of the black entertainer in the early years of films that it must be included in this story.

His real name was Egbert Austin Williams. He was born in Antigua in 1874 of African, Danish, Spanish, and West Indian ancestry. His grandfather was the Danish consul in Antigua. When he was eleven, his family moved to Riverside, California, where his father became a railroad conductor. He graduated from Riverside High School and spent one semester at Stanford.

Bert Williams wanted to be an entertainer. He dropped out of college and began to play the piano and sing in saloons and lumber camps. He was not a success and soon decided to concentrate on being a real "nigger entertainer." Blackening his light skin with burnt cork, he put on a wig, greasy red lipstick, and ragged clothes and began to develop the character of a comical coon. He shuffled, he mumbled, he stammered, he rolled his eyes.

He teamed up with the well-dressed dandy, George Walker, and they put together an act. Billing themselves as "The Two Real Coons," they worked their way east along the vaudeville circuit to New York, where they were booked into Koster and Bial's Music Hall, just months after Edison's first motion pictures were shown there.

Along Broadway that year the hit songs were "Every Race Has a Flag but the Coon," "He's Just a Little Nigger, but He's Mine, All Mine," and the most famous, "All Coons Look Alike to Me," written by Ernest Hogan, a black vaudevillian.

Williams was a brilliant pantomimist, trapped by the times behind his black-face mask. He often declared his ambition to "stop doing piffle and interpret the *real* Negro on the stage." But it never happened. He and Walker appeared in several hit musicals and in 1902 their show *In Dahomey* toured Europe, where they gave a command performance at Buckingham Palace. Then, after ten years of joint stardom, Walker died, and in 1910 Williams signed a contract to appear with star billing in the Ziegfield Follies.

But even a star was unable to forget the color of his skin. In her book *Nobody: A Biography of Bert Williams*, Ann Charters quotes a letter from Williams to a friend: "I was thinking about all the honors that are showered on me in the theatre, how everyone wishes to shake my hand or get an autograph. . . . However, when I reach a hotel, I am refused permission to ride on the passenger elevator, I cannot enter the dining room for my meals and am Jim Crowed generally. I am not complaining particularly . . . I am just wondering."

Williams was in a constant state of exile from the white world and, because he was a West Indian, from Harlem as well. As his biographer describes it, "The split between his public and private life weighed heavily on him and he began to suffer from a deep chronic depression.

Williams as he usually appeared onstage

But his inner melancholy only enriched his ability to make people laugh." W. C. Fields called him "the funniest man I ever saw and the saddest man I ever knew."

In 1914 Williams made four or five short one-reel films at the Biograph Film Studios in the Bronx. Charters writes: "These were offered 'to the trade' but according to an attorney for Biograph, all the companies to whom the films were offered decided the South would reject a Negro star." One recreated his most famous routine—the one-man poker game. Another, in which he played a black preacher terrified by a haunted graveyard, was shown on a 1963 television documentary as representing the worst kind of black stereotype.

In an interview in *Variety*, Williams discussed the play he planned for the 1927 season: "'I'm a porter in a hotel, an awful liar but a character. And I've got a song . . . that I sing to a gangling-legged outcast dog.

"'A lady has given me a dollar to take the dog out and feed him and her husband has given me five dollars to take the dog out and drown him.

"'I think I ought to be able to understand the way that old black porter feels. Yes,' he added in that mellow melancholy bass, 'and I think I ought to be able to understand how the dog feels too.'"

The play opened in Chicago. On stage one night, wearing his blackface mask, Bert Williams collapsed. Two weeks later he died, at the age of forty-seven, a weary, sad, black clown. Al Jolson and Irving Berlin were his pallbearers. Thousands of people followed his coffin through the streets of Harlem. The coffin was covered with blankets of orchids and white roses.

Above: Williams in his redcap costume
Below: Williams as he appeared in 1922, five years before his death

The Birth of a Nation

The Birth of a Nation was Hollywood's first spectacular. At a time when most films were one or two reels in length and produced in less than a week, *The Birth of a Nation* was rehearsed for six weeks, filmed in nine, and cost $100,000. In its final form it was twelve reels in length and ran for three hours.

Many of the filmmaking techniques still used today were introduced for the first time in this film—techniques such as night photography, moving camera shots, soft focus photography, lap dissolves, the split screen, and acute camera angles. Moreover, for the first time in films, the audience laughed, cried, feared, cheered, and *cared* about the people whose story was being told on the screen. It was the first fully realized story, and it evoked a full range of human emotions.

More than twenty-five million people saw it in the first two years after its release. In one city it played continuously for the next twelve years. At a time when most movies cost only a nickel, *The Birth of a Nation* cost two dollars. It earned millions for its financial backers and alerted big business to the fact that there was money to be made in the movies. Responses were widely varied but all highly emotional. After a White House showing, the first for any film, President Woodrow Wilson is reported to have said, "It is like writing history with lightning and my one regret is that it is all so terribly true."

The film pleased many, and even helped inject new life into a languishing Ku Klux Klan. But blacks, and others sensitive to the film's racial injustices, hated it. Riots and lawsuits resulted from its public screenings. When it opened at the Tremont Theatre in Boston, five thousand blacks marched on the state capitol, demanding it be banned. In Philadelphia its first showing resulted in fights involv-

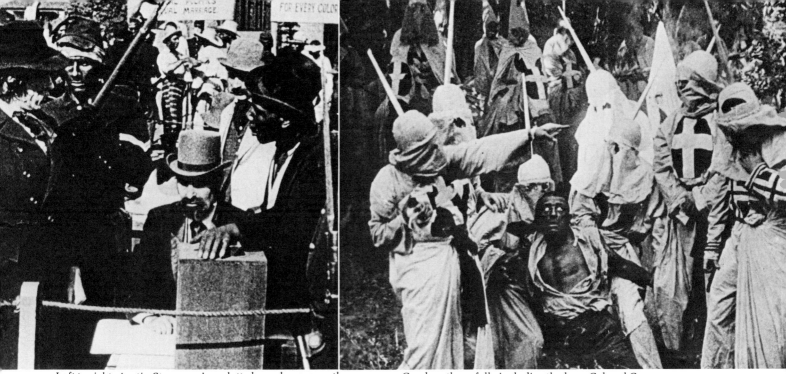

Left to right: Austin Stoneman's mulatto housekeeper seethes with fury after being snubbed by Senator Sumner; The "good southern mammy" confronts "de uppity nigger from de No' ";

Good southern folk, including the hero Colonel Cameron (foreground) are denied the right to vote; The heroic Ku Klux Klan in operation.

ing three thousand blacks.

Set in the period of the Civil War, the film traces the history of two families: the Camerons, aristocrats from the South, and the Stonemans, leading abolitionists from the North. Ben Cameron and Elsie Stoneman are about to marry when war breaks out. Ben Cameron, "the Little Colonel," is wounded in battle, captured, and about to be executed as a traitor. But the Stoneman family convinces Lincoln to intervene. Cameron is released and returns home to a South ravaged by defeat.

Meanwhile, Austin Stoneman is appointed advisor to Silas Lynch, the mulatto lieutenant governor of the Cameron's home state. Lynch, the villain, is plotting a black stranglehold on the South. When the rule of carpetbaggers begins, it brings with it a tyranny of black power. Swaggering black thugs brutalize whites and their women, denying them the right to vote and even to walk the streets in peace. A hideous "black empire" is being conceived, and only the intervention of an army of chivalrous heroes, the Ku Klux Klan, formed by "the Little Colonel," saves the day.

The creative genius behind the film, whose story is an adaptation of the Reverend Thomas Dixon's novel *The Clansmen*, was David Wark Griffith. Griffith was the son of "Roaring Jake" Griffith, a Kentucky colonel, a member of that state's legislature and a hero of the Confederacy. The war and its aftermath were tragic for the Griffiths, as for many southern families. Their fortune was wiped out and "Roaring Jake" died shortly thereafter, leaving them penniless. His son's deep feelings about the times remained vivid in his mind through the next fifty years.

That the history portrayed in the film was grossly distorted and that it maligned an entire race of people was never clear to Griffith, who made the film with all the artistry at his disposal. He was astonished at the storm of protest it aroused and at the accusation of "racial slander." Until he died, he defended his creation as truth.

After *The Birth of a Nation,* movies never again so blatantly portrayed the black as vicious brute, though this hardly compensated for the excesses of the film. Emmett J. Scott, who had been Booker T. Washington's secretary, considered filming a prologue to be tacked onto *The Birth of a Nation.* He then tried unsuccessfully to sell Universal a film scenario to be called *Lincoln's Dream.* Finally, he decided to make his own movie, which would be called *The Birth of a Race.* Three years in the making, twelve reels long, the film was financed by black investors. But when Scott ran out of money, he turned to a group of whites for help and was forced to make the changes they required. The result was a strange, garbled, uneven failure.

By this time, America's attention was diverted to the growing conflict in Europe which was to become World War I. To those blacks who questioned whether such a war deserved their support, DuBois wrote in *Crisis:* "We have more to gain from a society where democracy is at least an ideal than from one such as Nazi Germany." He urged wholehearted support.

Blacks were among the first to volunteer. Equality was theirs in terms of the numbers drafted, if not in the treatment they received. Colonel Charles Young, the highest-ranking black army officer, was retired from active duty on the grounds that his health was poor. The robust Colonel Young rode horseback from Ohio to Washington to demonstrate his fitness, but the ruling stood. Many have suggested that he was retired because the country was not ready for a black army general.

Southerners objected to blacks being trained in "their" army camps. Wherever they turned, black soldiers training to "make the world safe for democracy" were surrounded by Jim Crow laws and customs. Units of the armed forces were totally segregated, and no provisions were made for training black officers until, reluctantly yielding to pressure, the army established a black officer's training camp in Des Moines, Iowa. But New York's 369th Infantry, a black regiment, spent more time at the front than any other American unit.

During July of 1917, as blacks were fighting in Europe, other men were burned alive in their homes in East St. Louis because they were black. Six thousand others were driven out of town. Within just a few months, twenty-five race riots were recorded. In response to these riots and continued lynchings, fifteen thousand blacks took part in a silent parade in New York City. One large banner carried by marchers read, "We hold these truths to be self-evident that all men are created equal."

Partly because of *The Birth of a Nation,* the Ku Klux Klan had found new life. In 1915, beneath a fiery cross that burned on Stone Mountain near Atlanta, Imperial Wizard William J. Simmons declared that "other races *must* yield to the Anglo-Saxon." Eighty-three lynchings were recorded in 1919, and several of those lynched were veterans just returned from the war. That year, crosses burned in Indiana, New England, and throughout the South; more than two hundred public Klan meetings were held. The Grand Dragon of the Indiana Klan announced to the public, "*I* am the law in Indiana."

Then World War I was over. Weary of responsibilities and crusades, America wanted to hear no more of blood and bombs, riots and lynchings, the orphans and the poor. They wanted a party, a dream, a song.

Elmo K. Lincoln, the first Tarzan, and his Jane enjoy meeting a young savage in Tarzan (1920).

And Hollywood, maturing into America's Dream Factory, was learning to give them what they wanted. For white theatre audiences there were Mary Pickford, Douglas Fairbanks, Charlie Chaplin, Rudolph Valentino; the perfumed, opulent, silk-and-feathers domestic dreams of Cecil B. De Mille; the stories of cowboys, flaming youth, and the all-night party. For the black theatre audience? Nothing. The social message was clear despite Hollywood's protests to the contrary. Movies were becoming a giant corporate concern controlled by bankers and large investors who saw box office receipts as the only dependable index of what should be produced. "We are not moulders of opinion," they said. "We are here only to entertain. Our films carry no social message."

It became possible for a black actor to find work in Hollywood playing a butler or a maid. A few of them were comic servants in featured parts. The rest just passed the salad or opened the door. Then with the growing popularity of exotic location films came the "from darkest Africa" pictures. Blacks were hired as cannibals or savages—hired by the hundreds. Another old stereotype in a new loincloth!

Our Gang

In 1921 the successful Hollywood producer, Hal Roach, was searching for a subject for a series of film shorts, having already done two-reel slapstick comedies, melodramas, and bathing beauty parades. Some newspaper stories attributed the inspiration for his new series to "an afternoon frolic with his children"; and others to his "watching a group of children playing on a woodpile in the studio back lot."

However it came to him, the idea was to film a comedy series about the lives of children. It was named *Our Gang*, and the original gang consisted of Mickey Daniels, Jackie Condon, and "Sunshine Sammy." By the time the series got underway, "Sammy," who had appeared previously with Harold Lloyd in two-reel comedies, was almost a teenager. His replacement was just eighteen months old when Roach placed him under contract. His name was Allen Clayton Hoskins, but studio executives dubbed him "Farina," and dressed him in frayed old clothes, floppy shoes, and pickanniny pigtails tied up with rags. He remained with *Our Gang* until 1933 and later appeared in numerous Joe E. Brown films. In 1930 Matthew "Stymie" Beard of the shaved head and ever-present derby became a part of the gang and was joined two years later by Billy "Buckwheat" Thomas.

When Roach sold the rights to *Our Gang* to M-G-M in 1938, he retained ownership of the name, so that under M-G-M, the series was known as *The Little Rascals.* They continued to produce it until

Above: "Farina"

Above: "Stymie" and Pete the pup
Opposite: "Stymie" (left) greets "Farina."
Right: "Alfalfa," the cowboy, makes a traditional
gesture toward "Buckwheat," the Indian.

1944, when it was discontinued. During the twenties and thirties *Our Gang* represented the only film efforts that were in any way integrated. Black children and white children played naturally together as friends. Although the black children were sometimes cast as comic coons, frightened, pop-eyed, and often were the butt of the white children's jokes, the treatment of blacks in *Our Gang* was more fair than in any other film of the period.

In D. W. Griffith's One Exciting Night (1922) Romeo Washington, the trembling, pop-eyed, comic fool is played by Porter Strong in blackface.

Back in 1903, W. E. B. Dubois wrote in *The Souls of Black Folk,* "Am I an American or am I a Negro? Can I be both?" By 1920, the hopes raised by the rhetoric of World War I had been crushed, and masses of discouraged black people replied, "No!"

It was to these people that a man named Marcus Garvey, an exponent of the Back to Africa movement and black nationalism, made his appeal. "Up you mighty race!" Garvey cried in hundreds of speeches around the United States. "The hour of Africa's redemption cometh! One day, like a storm, it will be here!"

Garvey boasted of being a full-blooded black with not a trace of white blood. He dreamed of an international brotherhood of black men and "a new homeland in Africa." Black workers poured $10 million into the Garvey movement. In 1921, twenty-five thousand blacks from all over the world attended his Universal Negro Improvement Association's convention. Fifty thousand Garveyites paraded down Lenox Avenue behind Garvey, who wore a uniform of purple and gold and a helmet with feathers "as tall as Guinea grass."

White and black leaders alike denounced him as a demagogue and charlatan. The feeling was mutual. "The NAACP," Garvey wrote, "wants us to become white." In 1923 the United States government began investigation of Garvey's Black Star Line, founded to transport blacks back to Africa. He was tried and convicted for using the mails to defraud, spent two years in the Atlanta penitentiary, and was then deported to his native Jamaica.

Even after Garvey's exile, black nationalism continued to have its influence. In 1913, a man named Noble Drew Ali had founded the Moorish-American Science Temple, emphasizing a belief in Islam and teaching that blacks were Asiatic Moors. He died suddenly in 1929, and one year later a new prophet appeared. Master Wallace Fard Muhammed claimed to be Drew Ali reincarnated. He founded a Temple of Islam in Detroit and

Chicago, attracting many ex-Garveyites. When Fard disappeared in 1934 as mysteriously as he had appeared, his chief lieutenant, Elijah Muhammed, took his place.

It was the roaring twenties, an age of easy money and good times. A frank spirit of hedonism reigned. People wanted fast cars, strong whiskey, and all-night parties. They wanted to enjoy the pleasures of the dollar. F. Scott Fitzgerald, the high priest of the times, wrote, "America was going on the greatest, gaudiest spree in history." Prohibition made a game out of breaking the law and heroes out of those flashy, shadowy characters called bootleggers.

Prosperous whites in search of new forms of entertainment soon discovered Harlem after dark. In their evening clothes, they would come uptown on the subway to hear the music of Jelly Roll Morton, Duke Ellington, and Fats Waller. The Cotton Club and Connie's Inn packed them in night after night. The Jazz Age was born.

In Greenwich Village the Provincetown Playhouse, Eugene O'Neill, and black actor Charles Gilpin opened wide a new door in the American theatre when Gilpin played the leading role in *The Emperor Jones*.

In Harlem Claude McKay, Langston Hughes, and Countee Cullen read their poetry and both blacks and whites listened. Tenor Roland Hayes became the first black man to find acceptance as a serious concert artist. The Hall Johnson Choir revived the rich old folk melodies and toured the country. Novels, painting, sculpture, and music ranging from ragtime to symphonies were produced in this brilliant decade of the Harlem Renaissance.

In 1921 the all-black musical *Shuffle Along* had opened on Broadway, and soon everyone was singing "I'm Just Wild about Harry." It was followed by a succession of all-black reviews, such as *Runnin' Wild*, which gave the country the Charleston, then *Chocolate Dandies*, *Blackbirds*, *Hot Chocolates*, *Porgy and Bess*, and in 1930, the saga of "De Lawd" and his angels, *The Green Pastures*.

There were other advances as well. Oscar de Priest, elected in 1928 to represent Chicago's South Side, was the first black to serve in Congress since the turn of the century.

But with the economic squeeze of the late twenties, the Harlem Renaissance seemed to fade away. Whites were no longer interested; blacks were again out of work. 'Last hired, first fired" was a fact. And the income of sharecroppers living in the rural South was still no more than $300 a year.

The only black beneficiaries of the High Times of the twenties were the entertainers and musicians who made it to night clubs, Broadway, and finally to Hollywood. Meanwhile, back at the box office, the movie business was in a slump. Warner Brothers, a minor film studio with major money problems, decided on a desperate gamble. A device called Vitaphone added sound to film and, crude though it was, Warners staked their last pennies on the exclusive rights to it.

The Jazz Singer (1927) was their first "sound" feature—ordinary enough except for the addition of three Jolson songs and a bit of dialogue. Wherever the film was shown, long lines formed. Hollywood believed it was a short-lived novelty. But within a year, it was clear that the "talkies" would soon relegate silent films to the world of antiques.

Al Jolson in blackface sings "Mammy" in the first "talkie," The Jazz Singer (1927).

Hearts in Dixie and Hallelujah

Hollywood had a voice. It could talk. It could sing. It decided to dance. For years, the noted director King Vidor had been trying to persuade M-G-M to let him make a film with an all-black cast. Now that it was possible to make a musical film, Vidor argued, what more likely subject was there than those handclapping, toetapping, goodhearted simple folk, the black slaves? Studio executives agreed, and Vidor began work on *Hallelujah*, but not before a rival studio, Fox, was well into the production of their all-black musical, *Hearts in Dixie*.

Hearts in Dixie was begun as a film short, depicting minstrel men, revival meetings, and happy slaves romping in the cotton. But on the strength of the performance of Stepin Fetchit, until then a little-known feature player, it was expanded into a full-length film. Fetchit played "Gummy, the laziest colored gent below the Mason-Dixon line." The film also introduced Clarence Muse as the

Left: Stepin Fetchit watches while Bernice Pilot chops wood   Right: Happy pickanninies "deep in de cotton"

kindly Tom, Napus. Muse, a lawyer, songwriter ("When It's Sleepy Time Down South"), playwright, producer, and singer, went on to appear in over 200 movies.

Studio publicity promised moviegoers novel musical delights. "Hear 200 entertainers from the levees and cotton fields . . . billbrew chorus of 60 voices . . . weird voodoo ceremonies . . . plantation melodies. . . . See Hilarious Plantation Wedding in Crinoline Days . . . Real Old-Fashioned Southern Barbeque . . . The Good Ship Nellie Bly, Pride of the Mississippi." The music was beautiful, the dancing unrestrained and joyous, and the slaves shown as simpleminded and contented with their lot.

Hallelujah was somewhat more serious business. Vidor had originally planned the film to star Paul Robeson and Ethel Waters, but Robeson was unavailable and Vidor seems to have decided against Ethel Waters. Instead he selected Daniel Haynes, who had been an understudy in *Show Boat*, and Nina Mae McKinney, a seventeen-year-old Broadway chorus girl. M-G-M signed her to a five-year contract, but after *Hallelujah* there were no parts for her. She toured Europe as a singer, billing herself as "the Black Garbo," then starred in the British film, *Sanders of the River* (1935) with Paul Robeson. Later, she returned to the United States and appeared in several all-black independent films. Her last ap-

pearance was in *Pinky* (1949), in which she had a small part as a tough, razor-toting broad. She died during the 1960s, her talents totally unexplored; her career in many ways was a prototype of women such as Fredi Washington and Dorothy Dandridge—they were not mammies, not comics, but beautiful talented actresses.

Hallelujah is the story of a simple black boy gone wrong. In town to collect the earnings from his family's cotton picking, Zeke (Daniel Haynes) meets Chick (Nina Mae McKinney), the beautiful dancer and lady of easy virtue. He loses the family's money to Chick's gamblin' man, Hot Shot (William Fountaine), and accidentally shoots his brother, Spunk (Everett McGarrity). In repen-

tence, he becomes a revival preacher, and soon he becomes famous and successful and again encounters Chick. Moments after baptizing her, he is chasing her down the road, apparently having forgotten the hundreds of other petitioners waiting by the river. Chick lures him back into a life of sin, he kills her and Hot Shot, and ultimately returns, repentent, to the happy simple plantation life and his Mammy (Fannie Belle de Knight) and Pappy (Harry Gray).

Harry Gray, an ex-slave, newspaper editor, lecturer, minister, and author, was eighty-six years old when King Vidor approached him on the street in Harlem and offered him a part in the movies. The three little boys who played Zeke's

Left to right: Clarence Muse as Napus and a jubilant dance number from Hearts in Dixie;
Fanny Belle de Knight as Mammy and Harry Gray as Pappy with the children from Hallelujah;
Nina Mae McKinney, William Fountaine, and Daniel Haynes in Hallelujah.

younger brothers were also said to have been discovered in Harlem by Vidor. They were dancing on a Harlem street-corner for pennies.

The film was made on location in Louisiana and Arkansas. The world premiere was held simultaneously at the Embassy Theater in downtown New York and the Lafayette Theater in Harlem. Billed as Harlem's first world premiere and a great cultural achievement, the dual opening was seen by some as an attempt to Jim Crow blacks and keep them from coming downtown to see the film.

In both *Hearts In Dixie* and *Hallelujah*, blacks are represented as whites wished to portray them. Both films imply that the ideas of emancipation and equality must have come not from the southern blacks, but from busybodies from the North.

Left to right: Harry Gray as Pappy mourns the death of his son, Spunk; Nina Mae McKinney and Daniel Haynes

Stepin Fetchit

Stepin Fetchit feeds a seal in Big Time *(1929)*

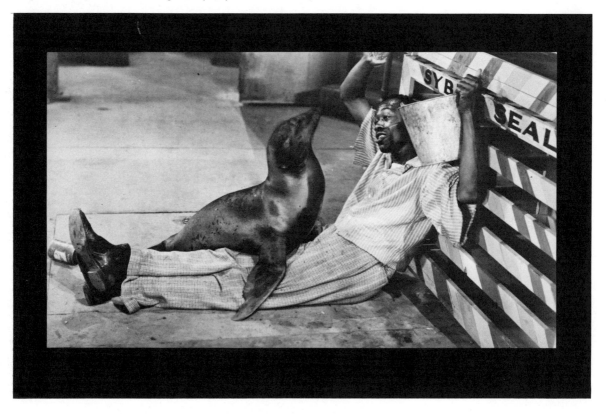

Stepin Fetchit has spent most of the last thirty years defending himself against charges of selling out his race and of playing the "arch coon" with such style and brilliance that he earned, and subsequently lost, millions of dollars.

His real name was Lincoln Theodore Monroe Andrew Perry—after four presidents. He took the name Stepin Fetchit from a horse which had won him some money during the time he was a medicine show performer. Inspired by the name, he wrote a song called "The Stepin Fetchit, Stepin Fetchit Turn Around, Stop and Catch It, Chicken Scratch It to the Ground Rag."

He soon graduated to vaudeville, then to Hollywood, where he appeared in several silent films. His first feature role, in *Hearts in Dixie,* brought him instant success. A *New York Times* article in 1933 said, "Fetchit accepted his fame in a gaudy African style which makes the antics of Brutus Jones pale into reticence by comparison."

Fetchit bought the biggest house on Central Avenue and three cars, including one pink Rolls Royce with his name in neon lights on the back, employed one liveried chauffeur for each car, owned over fifty suits—some which cost $2,000 each and some which were celebrity hand-me-downs bought from Rudolph Valentino's tailor after Valentino's death—bought tickets to boxing matches by the bunch because he liked to sit in

Stepin Fetchit with Warner Oland in Charlie Chan in Egypt (1935)

the center of a block of friends, and employed fourteen Chinese servants and one liveried footman—who wore a coat of many colors as he served him. His life was a press agent's dream, and certainly some of it a press agent's creation.

Some of the stories circulated about him described him as "temperamental and irresponsible." He complained continually about conditions on the set, insisted on doing some of his own directing, and, worst of all, would disappear during filming despite the efforts of studio detectives hired to keep track of him. Fox fired him after *The Prodigal* (1931), and he was forced to return to small-time vaudeville to reflect and repent.

During the next three years, the only good thing that happened to him, he claimed, was that Mrs. John Hay Whitney named a horse after *him*.

Fox took him back in 1934, and that year he appeared in nine movies. A newspaper article reported that "he now drives his own flivver, lives in a modest room and is saving his money, or rather the studio is saving it for him." Fetchit and Will Rogers were the most famous of the master-servant teams of the thirties. A look at their relationship casts light on the race relations of the times. Rogers

kicks Fetchit, he threatens Fetchit, he takes him in trade for a horse—all with the kind of condescending affection one offers a pet dog. Movie audiences loved it.

In the late thirties, Fetchit appeared in fewer and fewer pictures. And his troubles increased. Newspaper clippings report car accidents and a series of assault charges, all dismissed. He appeared in several films in the forties, but his movie career was largely over. Civil rights groups objected to his performances, his money was gone, and his reputation blemished.

It can be argued that despite the characterization he was given Fetchit was a great artist. His insistence on directing some of his own film sequences is an old-time echo of the demands now being made in the industry. As Fetchit put it in a recent interview in *Film Quarterly:* "People don't understand any more what I was doing then, least of all the young generation of Negroes. Maybe because they don't really know what it was like then. Hollywood was more segregated than Georgia. . . . Humor is my only alibi for being here. Show business is a mission for me . . . I was a 100% black accomplishment."

Left: Robert Young and Stepin Fetchit in Carolina (1934)   Below: Stepin Fetchit and the horse are a package deal, taken in trade by Will Rogers in David Harum (1934).

Oscar Micheaux and the Black Independents

During the period of the Harlem Renaissance in the late twenties, about 700 movie theatres in the United States catered specifically to blacks. A few movie companies were formed to make films especially for this audience: Ebony Films in Chicago, Gate City Films in Kansas City, and Colored Players Film Corporation in Philadelphia produced all-black films. None of these companies seem to have survived the Depression and little is known about them, although prints of a few films are still in existence.

More important and long-lasting in its influence was the work of a man named Oscar Micheaux. A one-man movie company, Micheaux made his first film, *The Homesteader,* an adaptation of his own novel, in 1918; his last, *The Betrayal,* in 1948; and at least thirty others in between. Micheaux began with little money and never sought investments by financial backers. Instead, he would set out each year, armed with copies of his script and photographs of the actors who were to appear in it. Traveling around the country he would persuade theatre owners to book the film and pay him in advance. He would return to Harlem to make the film, usually in a matter of months, then go back on the road to distribute it. This procedure followed a successful system he developed as a novelist, when he formed his own company to publish his books and traveled to black communities around the country to promote and sell them. When he shifted to filmmaking, his merchandising pattern remained unchanged.

The financing was never easy and the limitations it imposed are reflected in the quality of his films. Micheaux was extremely cost-conscious and would rarely reshoot a scene, no matter how badly it turned out. He economized on sets, the number of technicians he hired, and the time devoted to shooting and editing. He filmed in friends' homes or offices rather than in studios, hired actors who would work cheap, and acted as his own director.

The stories were often typically Hollywood—adventures, melodramas, mysteries—starring black actors. There was little "ethnic truth" to these films; Micheaux gave his audiences "a black Valentino" and a "sepia Mae West." And he perpetuated many white stereotypes; his heroes and heroines were usually light-skinned and fine-featured, his villains darker and more Negroid. While some of his films dealt with the problems of being black, this was never from the point of view of the ghetto dweller or sharecropper; his subjects were the black bourgeoisie. By presenting them, Micheaux hoped to instill race pride in all who saw them. His attitude was not unlike the

Belafonte-Poitier integrationists who followed him, though his energy in seeking out "his audience" and his total control over the financing of his films was much like that of Melvin Van Peebles.

In 1922 Micheaux made a film called *The Dungeon*, a seven-reel melodrama. The American Film Institute catalogue gives the following description, quoted from the New York State film license records: "The story treats of Gyp Lassiter, a villainous wretch who employs a drug fiend to hypnotize a woman whom he wants to get possession of. The drug fiend brings the woman to Gyp who marries her while she is in a hypnotic condition. Gyp then takes her to a house which has been the scene of the murder of eight of his previous wives. By nature a killer, he then proceeds to asphyxiate her in a dungeon. From the clutches of death, she is rescued by a former lover who then kills Gyp." His later films become less melodramatic, and more powerful. *Birthright* (1924), *Body and Soul* (1925), with Paul Robeson, and *God's Stepchildren* (1937) are among his most interesting.

During the thirties and forties, Jack Goldberg, Jed Buell, and Ted Toddy all produced films for black audiences, including *Mystery in Swing*, *Paradise in Harlem*, *Harlem on the Prairie*, *Murder on Lenox Avenue*, *Lucky Ghost*, *Boogie Woogie Dream*, *Reet, Petite and Gone*, *Ebony Parade*, *Sepia Cinderella*, and *Bronze Venus*. All three men were white and their films, unlike those of Micheaux, were generally condescending and exploitative. But many of them nevertheless are full of the fun and raw energy invested in them by talented players who enjoyed making movies.

Micheaux's last movie, *The Betrayal*, opened in a "white" movie theatre in downtown New York. The reviews were poor. Three years later, Micheaux died, still largely an unknown. The end of the all-black independents coincided almost exactly with the time Hollywood began its 1949 "racial problem" film cycle. It is doubtful that the death of one was a direct result of the birth of the other, but it was the beginning of the integrationist age.

Left: A scene from Bronze Buckaroos, an all-black Western
Right: Webster and Sappho Dill in Melancholy Dame, a 1929 all-black production.

In October 1929 the financial boom, which had seemed infinitely expanding, was suddenly over. For those who had once had money, there were now only hard times. For those who had been "getting along," there was now starvation. Long lines of thin, exhausted people waited to receive a slice of stale bread or watery soup; ragged children with matchstick arms and bloated bellies rummaged through garbage cans for food, competing with dogs and cats. A pathetic assortment of tin and cardboard shanties appeared in every city; called "Hoovervilles," they were named in honor of the stiff, plodding president who tried to help but denounced the "dole."

The decade that opened with the Great Depression and closed with the sound of gunfire in Europe brought some blacks and whites closer together. In 1932 an army of unemployed war veterans, both black and white and numbering almost twenty thousand, descended on Washington demanding a bonus. They set up their "Hooverville" within sight of the White House and ultimately were routed by the U.S. army led by General Douglas MacArthur. While their protest lasted, the "bonus marchers" found a certain solidarity that transcended skin color. In the South, black and white tenant farmers united to demand more than the $300 to $400 they were able to earn each year.

A spirit of compassion seemed to exist between poor men. But the relationships of blacks to labor unions and large corporations did not improve. Jobs, when there were jobs, went to white men. Black businesses sold out or closed up, eliminating one more source of black employment. Sharecroppers whose land was gone poured into the cities in search of work, crowding the already desperate and jobless city dwellers, until ghettos like Harlem were packed with sick, neglected, and hopeless human beings. In 1932 Harlem Hospital, which cared for the health needs of 350,000 people had only 273 beds. Blacks who referred to it as "the butcher shop" preferred to die at home.

Although there was no work for their men, black women could work if they were not at all particular about what they did and grateful for the slave wages they received. Several streetcorners in the Bronx were known as the "slave market." Harlem women gathered there every day in any weather to be hired as housemaids at ten or twenty cents an hour. In the South a washerwoman could usually earn fifty cents for washing and ironing a basketful of clothes—a backbreaking day's labor.

Looking back at the movies of the thirties, it is impossible to tell that a depression was going on. Anyone who had twenty-five cents to spend could "escape" to the beckoning arms of slinky Jean Harlow or the "brazen hussy" Mae West; to the robust world of Clark Gable or Gary Cooper; into the dreamy paradise of Nelson Eddy and Jeanette MacDonald singing nose-to-nose; or Fred Astaire and Ginger Rogers patting, tapping, and twirling across polished floors.

The studios believed that escape was what the people wanted and what it profited them to provide. They were taking no chances. And so when a giant black man with multiple talents and great dignity came knocking at their door, he found it closed—and locked.

Paul Robeson

One night in the spring of 1959, an aging Paul Robeson took command of the Shakespeare Theatre's stage at Stratford-on-Avon. As he began Othello's speech, "I have given the state some service . . ." applause broke out among the usually staid British audience, and when the performance was over he received thirteen long, loving curtain calls. In his sixty-first year, after ten years of having been denied the right to travel outside the United States, after ten years when all American stage doors had been closed to him and efforts had been made to erase the very fact of his existence, Paul Robeson again had a voice.

The son of slavery, the first black All-American football player, scholar, lawyer, the man for whom Jerome Kern wrote "Ole Man River," Eugene O'Neill's Hairy Ape, the movies' Emperor Jones, an international hero and spokesman for the world's oppressed, Paul Robeson had been since 1950 the victim of a boycott of organized silence.

From the beginning of his career in the twenties, he had fought for a reasonable and honest black image on the stage and on the screen. In 1933, when he and two independent producers proposed a film version of O'Neill's *The Emperor Jones*, no Hollywood studio was interested. The film was made independently. Between 1934 and 1940 he made a series of films in England, where he had gone to live. The films were disappointing, and Robeson

Paul Robeson as Brutus Jones, the Pullman porter who becomes an emperor, and Dudley Diggs as Smithers, his white sidekick. The Emperor Jones (1933) was the first movie in which a black man was shown as dominant to a white man.

grew disillusioned with the colonialist attitude of upper-class Britons. He had developed an interest in his African heritage and in working-class people around the world.

In 1934 he visited the Soviet Union. As his interest in politics and economics grew, so did his admiration for the Soviet way of life. His son Paul attended school there for two years.

Returning to the United States to live, he devoted himself to his concert career and political activities. During World War II, he was known as a leading antifascist, and after the war people saw him drifting toward Marxism. In 1948 he declared, "I am a radical and am going to stay a radical." His appearance at a concert in Peekskill, New York, provoked riots. New York papers ran the story on the front page for days.

In 1950 NBC canceled his appearance on Eleanor Roosevelt's weekly television show because he was "too controversial." Shortly afterward his passport was withdrawn. Although a passport is not usually required for travel to Canada, on his way to Vancouver to sing and speak at a union meeting in 1952, he was turned back at the border "in the best interests of the United States government." Union members responded by moving the concert to Peace Arch Park, which spans the border between Washington

Robeson and Nina Mae McKinney in Sanders of the River (1935)

state and British Columbia. Thirty thousand Canadians came to hear and applaud Robeson. But when the World Federation of Trade Unions asked him to record the sound track of their film *Song of the Rivers,* Robeson was unable to rent any commercial recording studio and was forced to make the record in his brother's basement.

An eight-year fight and a Supreme Court ruling finally won him back his passport in 1958. He lived in England until 1963, when, in poor health and exhausted by long years of struggle, he returned to live in retirement in the United States.

Above: Robeson as Captain Joe in Shoe Boat *(1936)*
Right: Robeson and Ethel Waters find a coat filled with money in Tales of Manhattan *(1942). After making the film, Robeson refused to appear in any other Hollywood movie.*

The thirties were drab, sad years. After the stock market crash there were massive job layoffs, and finally the entire U.S. banking system failed. Black families imprisoned in the ghetto or on farms were the hardest hit. In the months after the Home Relief Office opened in 1933, half of Harlem's residents were on relief, and by 1935 nearly two-thirds of the nation's employable black people needed some form of public assistance.

Even the alms of charity were not always available to blacks. They were turned away from some soup kitchens. But a leader named Father Divine, a bald, cheerful man who claimed he was "God made flesh," took them under his heavenly wing. During those days of hunger his churches, called "heavens," invited crowds of blacks to free fried-chicken dinners. Father Divine preached thrift, cleanliness, and self-reliance. He set up a series of cooperative businesses—food stores, restaurants, coal yards, barbershops—where goods were available at just above cost. He set up a series of cooperative communities in which members shared their resources, with no regard to color. None of his followers were on relief and none went without food.

With the election of Franklin Delano Roosevelt to the presidency in 1932, the black at last had a friend in the White House. In the next hundred days, they watched the tough-minded Roosevelt push measure after measure through Congress: Roosevelt called it the New Deal. These new laws and the alphabet of agencies they created brought relief and recovery to white as well as black, and for the first time since Reconstruction days, the government was urging equal opportunity for blacks. The Works Progress Administration (WPA) offered jobs constructing roads, bridges, dams, public buildings, even hospitals, for blacks and buildings for black colleges; the Civilian Conservation Corps (CCC) camps offered young men a chance to escape the ghetto, earn their own way, and learn a trade; the National Recovery Administration (NRA) promised fair wages and working hours; the National Youth Administration (NYA) provided educational programs for large numbers of blacks; and the Federal Writers' Project (FWA) established programs for writers, artists, and actors.

Roosevelt restored America's confidence in itself. People began to swing to the music of Benny Goodman's clarinet and

Tommy Dorsey's trombone, they danced the Big Apple and the Lindy Hop; café society flourished, pouring money into El Morocco, the Stork Club, and "21"; Vanderbilts married Toppings; Barbara Hutton divorced Prince Mdivani for Count von Haugwitz-Reventlow; and Elsa Maxwell, Walter Winchell, and Louella Parsons breathlessly reported every juicy tidbit. Kate Smith reminded the nation that the moon comes over the mountain; Jack Benny sold it Jell-O and shouted for Rochester. And that dimpled, golden-curled, little Shirley Temple brought the very essence of sweetness and light back into people's lives.

Above: Five years after Hallelujah, *King Vidor directed* So Red the Rose *(1935). Daniel Haynes appeared as the faithful butler, William. After viewing the film, Haynes left Hollywood for good.   Below: Lionel Hampton (left) with the Benny Goodman Band in* Hollywood Hotel *(1937), the first "integrated" band to appear in the movies.*

Bill
"Bojangles"
Robinson

When "Bojangles" died in 1949, they carried his body through the streets of Harlem and down to Times Square. One million people lined the route, tipping their hats to the black man who had brought them a smile during the bad times of the Depression.

He was born Luther Robinson in Richmond, Virginia, in 1878. Raised by his grandmother, he left school at the age of seven after deciding he didn't belong there. At about the same time he decided he wanted to exchange names with his brother Bill. The two boys fought over the name. Luther won and changed his name to Bill, and Bill thereafter became Percy.

When he was eight he ran away to Washington, where he became a dancing pickaninny in a colored minstrel show. He supplemented his living by tap-dancing in saloons, selling newspapers, shining shoes, and later as a stable boy at a race track near Washington.

During the Spanish-American War Robinson tried to join a black regiment and was rejected, but he went along anyway. He came through the war unhurt only to be shot in the leg by an officer in a North Carolina dance hall.

One morning, after having been the big winner in an all-night poker game, Robinson celebrated the sunrise by tap-danc-

Above: Bill "Bojangles" Robinson with Will Rogers and Dorothy Wilson in In Old Kentucky
(1927)   Opposite left: Robinson and "his favorite pupil" do the famous stair dance in
The Little Colonel *(1935)   Opposite right: Robinson (center) with Eddie "Rochester" Anderson (left) and Fredi Washington (right) in* One Mile from Heaven *(1938).*

ing up and down an empty city street. "He's Bojangles, he is!" one of his friends cried. And "Bojangles," which Robinson said means happy-go-lucky, he became. At that time he was making a living by drifting along in small-time vaudeville and minstrel shows with odd jobs in between. In 1908, while working as a waiter at the Jefferson Hotel in Richmond, he accidentally spilled a bowl of oyster stew on a man named Marty Forkins. When the manager apologized to Forkins, explaining that Robinson was really a dancer and not a waiter, Forkins asked to see him dance, and immediately offered to be his manager. They remained together for the next forty years.

Robinson soon became a headliner in vaudeville, earning up to $3,500 a week. In 1927 he appeared in Lew Leslie's *Blackbirds* on Broadway. In one of his routines he danced up and down a flight of stairs, and soon the Bojangles "stair dance" became so famous that other dancers began to copy it. He took a full-page ad in a theatrical paper warning dancers to "keep off his routine." He later made a movie of the dance with the intention of trying to patent it, but the U.S. Patent Office denied his request. Vaudevillian Fred Stone once sent him a check for $1,500 for "the dance I stole

from you."

Robinson became the idol of Harlem. He was made Honorary Mayor. Everyone uptown knew his chauffeur-driven Duesenberg limousine with the license plate BR 6. And everyone knew what a soft touch he was. He gave money to any and every charity, no matter what it was—if it was for charity, Bill Robinson supported it. He donated over a million dollars to various causes and raised another three million in benefits, often appearing three or four times in one night.

He had a special love for police and fire departments, and they often called on him for money or special help. Wherever he went, he carried a gold-inlaid, pearl-handled revolver in an alligator skin holster, a diamond-studded case enclosing a badge which proclaimed him a deputy sheriff of the New York Police Department, and a pocketful of badges and courtesy cards from the police departments of hundreds of other cities.

He seemed tireless, ageless, and joyfully optimistic. He was the world champion of backward running, ate eight quarts of vanilla ice cream every day, and at age sixty-two celebrated his birthday by tap-dancing sixty-two blocks down Broadway. On the anniversary of his fiftieth year in show business, Harlem celebrated with a huge party at the Cotton Club. Dozens of celebrities sang and danced for him, and in return he danced for them, calling himself the Rip van Winkle of tap-dancing. He lived to dance for ten more years and when he died at age seventy-one, looking half his age, he had danced to the end. Among the gifts he left behind was a brand-new word for the English language. The word was "copacetic" and Webster's dictionary defines it as "capital, snappy, and prime."

Robinson and Willie Best, once known as "Sleep 'n Eat," watch Shirley Temple pass the cake in The Littlest Rebel *(1935).*

Louise Beavers

In Imitation of Life (1934), Louise Beavers as Delilah refuses a share in the joint pancake business Claudette Colbert offers her, asking only to be given "the biggest funeral Harlem ever did see."

Louise Beavers was born in Cincinnati and raised in Pasadena, California. Having decided to be an actress, she chose to try her luck in Hollywood rather than New York because "Hollywood was closer." Once there, she worked as a bit player and finally landed a part as a maid in a picture starring Lilyan Tashman. She played her part so capably that the star asked her to be her maid in real life. Louise Beavers accepted provided she might have time off if movie work came up. She was soon able to exchange her real-life maid's work for that of a movie maid.

She appeared in *Annabelle's Affairs* in 1931 and a dozen of the same in 1932. She was Mae West's maid in *She Done Him Wrong* (1933) and Jean Harlow's in *Bombshell* (1933). Many thought her performance in *Imitation of Life* (1934) deserved an Oscar nomination. In that movie, as in all her others, she was the loving loyal black mammy and the family cook who conjures up all sorts of delectable southern-fried goodies. The slow southern drawl, part and parcel of the character, did not come naturally to her—she worked hard to develop it. Equally unnatural was the full-bosomed, rounded figure Hollywood considered proper for the Aunt Jemima stereotype.

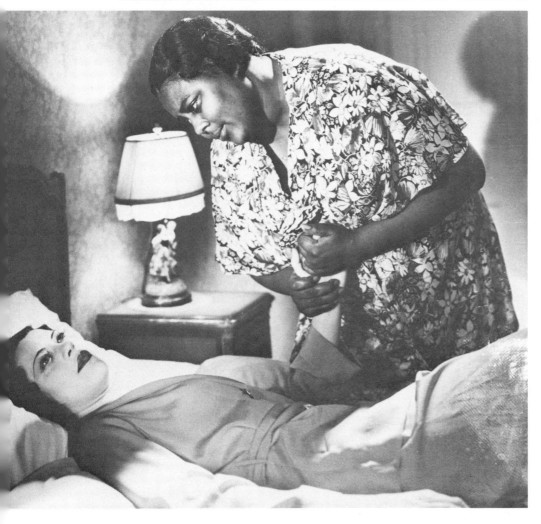

Left: Louise Beavers as the ex-slave Toinette in Rainbow on the River (1936). Bobby Breen co-stars.
Below: Delilah comforts her daughter Peola (Fredi Washington) who wants to "pass for white" in Imitation of Life (1934).

She had to work at gaining weight, force-feeding herself and often wearing padding and extra petticoats.

She won an important part in *Rainbow on the River* (1936) as Toinette, an ex-slave who did not value her own freedom and whose selfless love for a little white boy orphaned by the war was made totally believable by the strength of her performance. She then appeared in two or three films a year into the middle forties, including *Wings Over Honolulu* (1937), *Made for Each Other* (1939), *Virginia* (1941), *Holiday Inn* (1942), and *Barbary Coast Gent* (1944). As the ever-smiling black cook in *Mr. Blandings Builds His Dream House* (1948), by thinking up a zingy slogan for a baked ham account,

she saves advertising executive Cary Grant's job and his house. As a reward she is given a ten-dollar raise.

In 1950 she played Jackie Robinson's mother in *The Jackie Robinson Story*. Though she is not the one in uniform in this picture, the character she plays is largely unchanged. She appeared in *Never Wave at a Wac* (1953), *Tammy and the Bachelor* (1957), *All the Fine Young Cannibals* (1960). On television, she took her turn playing the title role in *Beulah*, following Hattie McDaniel and Ethel Waters. Her last film was *Facts of Life* (1961); she died in 1962. In the book *The Negro in Films*, Peter Noble calls her film career "a striking example of wasted talent."

Louise Beavers and Carole Lombard in Made for Each Other *(1939)*

Early in 1931, a fight broke out on a freight train bound for Alabama carrying several groups of boys "riding the rails" in search of work, blacks against whites. The white boys lost and jumped off. A posse was waiting at the next station, having been alerted by the white boys; the black boys were taken off the train, roped together, and taken to jail in a town named Scottsboro, Alabama. Later they were charged with the rape of two white girls who had also been on the train. Eight of the nine were convicted and sentenced to death. The youngest was just thirteen. News of the Scottsboro boys spread, along with the flimsiness of the evidence which had convicted them. The cases were tried and retried all the way to the Supreme Court. None was executed but all served long years in jail for what newspapers have called "the biggest frame-up of the century."

In 1934 the all-black road company of *The Green Pastures* was appearing in Washington. The management denied requests from blacks to alter the theatre's policy of excluding blacks. An actor named Johnny Logan, who played one of the Angels, attempted to lead the rest of the cast in a one-night protest strike, and that night the theater was surrounded by police and detectives. "De Lawd" spoke to the cast, explaining that the strike would only harm black folks. The management agreed. Only Johnny Logan remained determined. As he was hauled off to jail by detectives, onlookers report that he cried. The show went on.

Opposite: Rex Ingram as "De Lawd"   Above: Oscar Polk as the Angel Gabriel

The Green Pastures

In 1936 Warner Brothers decided to bring the long-running Broadway musical, *The Green Pastures,* to the screen. Adapted from the Roark Bradford sketches, "Ole Man Adam and His Chillun," the play had been written by Marc Connelly, and it was to Connelly that Warners entrusted the responsibility for the story of "De Lawd and His Heben."

One newspaper account of the time reflects the prevailing attitude of the public. This reports: "Connelly's heaven was built on Warner Sound Stage #8. It was to be a typical Southern picnic ground, with wide stretches of green field, running brooks, moss-hung trees and fleecy clouds substantial enough for angels to ride on. Tons of earth were poured over the reinforced floors. Huge trees were planted festooned with moss. Half an acre of sod was transplanted to the set. A running brook boasting real catfish was provided.

"Connelly designed this heaven as he found it visualized in the minds of the simple Southern Negro. What could be more understandable than that these people would picture Heaven as a place where a great fish fry could be celebrated throughout eternity?"

The story is framed in prologue and epilogue by a Sunday school class being taught by the kindly old preacher, the Reverend Deshee. As he describes it to his class, "De Lawd" creates the world as a place to drain off surplus "firmament" and orders the sun to commence shining to "dry my cherubs wings." Thereafter, he has to deal with the problems of Adam, of Noah, of Moses, and finally a delicate mention of Jesus.

The film was made in ten weeks, and in its final version runs for one hour and thirty-two minutes. There are one hundred eleven speaking parts, the largest number in any film to that date. Connelly cast many of the leading roles with actors from the Broadway production. But "De Lawd," Richard B. Harrison, had died shortly before the filming was to begin. Connelly worried over who might play the role. He considered Harrison's understudy, he considered Paul Robeson, he even considered Al Jolson. Finally, he settled on the actor who had been hired to play Adam, Rex Ingram.

A graduate of Northwestern University and a licensed physician, Rex Ingram was born on board the steamboat *Robert E. Lee*, where his father was fireman, in 1896. Before *The Green Pastures* he played mostly African savages, and though he appeared in many other films afterward, it is as "De Lawd" that he is best remembered. Ingram earned $1,000 a week. A few of the supporting players

"GANGWAY. Gangway for De Lawd God Jehovah." The heavenly fish fry is about to begin.

were also well-paid, but most of the cast, residents of Los Angeles, were paid just $4 to $7.50 a day.

In addition to Ingram as "De Lawd," the movie featured Oscar Polk, Eddie "Rochester" Anderson, Frank Wilson, Ernest Whitman, William Cumby, Edna Mae Harris, Al Stokes, David Bethea, George Reed, Clinton Rosemond and the Hall Johnson Choir, whose usual thirty voices were augmented by another forty. A *New York Times* article described the end of filming this way: "The Green Pastures Company is breaking up and it is an exodus unlike any other that the town has witnessed. Instead of waiting for fame to beckon from another studio, now that the drama is in the cuttingroom, the players are returning to their Pullman cars, their kitchens, and their chauffeur uniforms. The King of Babylon has gone into burlesque on Los Angeles' Main Street, the Angel Gabriel is returning to Harlem to rehearse a revue and the Archangel of Heaven is back on his run on the Santa Fe's Chief."

Twenty-five spirituals were sung in the film. When the children of Israel cross the Jordan to enter the land of Canaan, they sing "Joshua Fit de Battle of Jericho," when Noah sets out on the ark with his family, they sing "De Ole Ark's a Moverin', Moverin', Moverin'," when Moses demands the Israelites be released from bondage, they sing "Let My Chillun Go," and on the long weary walk out of Egypt they sing "I'se No Way Tired."

Left: Visiting the Earth, "De Lawd" tweaks the ear of Boy Gambler, played by Jazzlips Richardson, Jr.
Right: Eddie "Rochester" Anderson as a worried Noah

Eddie "Rochester" Anderson

When Eddie Anderson was twelve years old, he got a job peddling the *San Francisco Bulletin* at the foot of Market Street. Competition was fierce and the boy had to shout so loud he earned himself what he later described as "the world's biggest case of permanent laryngitis."

His father was a blackface minstrel and his mother a former circus tightrope walker. And Eddie wanted to go into show business. His mother discouraged him, saying, "It's only good if you're a headliner."

"Then I'll be a headliner," he reports having said, and he began performing in dance halls. When he was fourteen he landed a job in the chorus of *Struttin' Along*, then joined an all-black revue starring Edith Sterling. Later he, his brother Cornelius, and a friend put to-

Left: Jack Benny and Eddie "Rochester" Anderson in Love Thy Neighbor (1940)
Right: Andy Devine, Jack Benny, and Anderson in Buck Benny Rides Again (1940)

gether a song-and-dance act, billed themselves as "The Three Black Aces," and played small-time vaudeville.

He went east to tour the Loew's vaudeville circuit in 1929, but by the early thirties he was back in Hollywood, playing bits in movies. He appeared in *What Price Hollywood?* (1932) and *Rainbow on the River* (1936). His first feature role was that of Noah in *The Green Pastures* (1936), a role which he repeated with great success on television in 1959.

While performing at the Cotton Club Anderson was called to audition for the Jack Benny radio show. Benny hired him to play a railroad porter named Roches-

ter van Jones on the 1937 Easter Sunday show. It was to have been a one-time appearance. Anderson earned fifty dollars. But the audience and Benny like the banjo-eyed, gravel-voiced comic, so the "van Jones" was dropped, his salary increased, and he was made a permanent part of the cast. It was not long before the querulous call "R-O-C-H-E-S-T-E-R" and the croaking reply, "Coming, Mr. Benny!" had become one of radio's most famous exchanges.

In 1939 the Benny-Rochester team went to Hollywood, where they appeared in *Man About Town* with Dorothy Lamour and Phil Harris, then in *Buck Benny*

Left: *June Allyson and Anderson in* The Sailor Takes a Wife *(1945)*
Right: *June Havoc, Dennis O'Keefe, and Anderson in* Brewster's Millions *(1945)*

Rides Again (1940), *Love Thy Neighbor* (1940), and *The Meanest Man in the World* (1943). Speaking of Benny, Anderson said, "He's had my interest at heart all the way. He's a fine man to work with and has spent a lot of time developing me."

The little man with the big cigar whose ever-present hat ranged from a broad-brimmed fedora to a beret to an English boater found himself earning top money. During World War II, he owned a parachute factory and later a stable of race horses, a collection of cars, a boat, and a twelve-room house containing an auditorium, dance floor, and space for his extensive model railroad collection. A newspaper article written in 1941 reported that he had three valets of his own, named Crouch, Kicks, and Rowel.

More movie appearances followed, with vaudeville tours sandwiched in between. A typical vaudeville act consisted of a comedy skit between "Rochester" and an off-stage actor impersonating Benny or sometimes Fred Allen, a dance segment in which he did the shuffle dance, and a comic song or two such as "Janitor Man." In 1942 he starred as Little Joe in *Cabin in the Sky*, and his own blend of comedy and brooding melancholy made it a memorable performance. After *The Show-Off* (1946) he retired from the movies, returning only once for a brief appearance in *It's a Mad, Mad, Mad, Mad World* in 1963.

At the height of his fame Anderson said, "Sometimes people ask me why I don't have the frog in my throat operated on. Shucks man, that's a gold-plated frog."

Gone with the Wind

On the first night of shooting the film *Gone with the Wind* there was a fire—but it was intentional rather than accidental. The sets from four completed movies which stood on the M-G-M back lot were altered slightly to look like a southern city of the late 1800s. After the Los Angeles Fire Department was alerted, the sets were put to the match. The result, which lit up the sky all around Los Angeles, was the famous "burning of Atlanta" scene from the film.

Driving through it in a wagon were Scarlett O'Hara, Rhett Butler, Melanie Wilkes and her baby, and Prissy the slave girl. All parts were played by stand-ins. In fact, the actress who was to play Scarlett hadn't yet been found. (Legend has it that David O. Selznick's brother brought Vivien Leigh to meet Selznick that very night as he stood watching "Atlanta" burn, saying, "I've found your Scarlett.") Selznick had been searching for Scarlett in a well-publicized talent hunt for over a year. The film had been in the planning stages for two years. Still, the night that shooting began, fewer than half the scenes had been scripted.

The film, an adaptation of Margaret Mitchell's best-selling novel, cost a total of $4 million to produce. Selznick hired and then fired thirteen scriptwriters and three directors. All of them have left some small mark on the completed film, but the determination behind the mammoth production, the driving, unifying force, was that of Selznick himself. A total of 475,000 feet of film was shot and fi-

Opposite: Scarlett and Melanie are confronted by Belle Watling as Uncle Peter (Eddie "Rochester" Anderson) looks on.

Left: Vivien Leigh and Butterfly McQueen.
Right: Oscar Polk as Pork.

nally cut to 25,000—or three and three-quarter hours of movie. As screen epic it was second only to *The Birth of a Nation*. It premiered in Atlanta almost a year to the day after filming had begun, and the day of the premier was declared a state holiday.

Gone with the Wind is a story of the life and loves of Scarlett O'Hara during and after the Civil War in Georgia. Although many of the characters fall into the familiar movie Old South stereotype, most have a richness that rises above stereotype. While this is true for the characters of Mammy (Hattie McDaniel) and Prissy (Butterfly McQueen), the other black feature players, Oscar Polk, Everett Brown, and Eddie Anderson, do not fare as well. Anderson's part was so lifeless

and his usual sparkle hidden so far beneath make-up that few people even recognized him as Uncle Peter, Aunt Pittipat's coachman.

Very little of the $4 million budget was spent on actor's salaries. In fact, the entire cast of supporting players from Hattie McDaniel on down were paid a total of $10,000, a figure which almost equaled the cost of laundering the cast's costumes during the filming. Still, for Hattie McDaniel and Butterfly McQueen, the roles were the most important they were to have during their entire movie careers. And for Hattie McDaniel, *Gone with the Wind* meant an Oscar, the first a black person had received, and the last, for the next thirty years to come.

Above: After the war, Scarlett meets Big Sam (Everett Brown) on an Atlanta street.
Below: Hattie McDaniel and Clark Gable

Hattie McDaniel

Hattie McDaniel, Hollywood's memorable black mammy, was once a real-life maid. But not for long. At the age of twenty-six, after having been in show business for ten years, after having been the first black woman to sing on the radio, after having toured with Professor George Morrison's black orchestra and with the road company of *Show Boat,* she found herself in Milwaukee, out of a job and with no prospects.

She found work as a ladies-room maid in Sam Parks' Suburban Inn and waited. Given a chance to pinch-hit for an ailing singer, she took the stage, belted out "St. Louis Blues," and found herself the star of the floor show. Two years later she arrived in Hollywood and supported herself by playing bit parts in movies. In her first supporting role, *The Story of Temple Drake* (1933), she was cast as a maid. And a maid she remained—for over three hundred movie roles. When in March 1939 she won an Academy Award as Best Supporting Actress in *Gone with the Wind,* civil rights groups who had protested the filming of Margaret Mitchell's strongly pro-southern novel asked her to turn it down. She refused, saying, "I'd rather play a maid than be one."

Hattie McDaniel was born in Wichita, Kansas, in 1898, the thirteenth child of a Baptist preacher and his wife, a singer of spirituals. When she was fifteen, she won a drama medal from the white Woman's

Christian Temperance Union in Denver for her recitation of "Convict Joe."

As a fiercely protective, hard-to-please, devoted black mammy, she was the first to "talk back," thus defining herself as a human being. Although the standards she defended so fiercely were applied only to her masters and never to herself, although she seemed to have no life or desires other than to serve, the great talent and spirit of Hattie McDaniel overshadowed the parts written for her. Those who watched her knew that hidden behind the mammy was a real person. She once told an interviewer that "she would prize more than any other reward, a chance to appear in a singing picture. She would like to prove that she can do a blues number with the best of them."

She appeared on the *Amos 'n Andy Show*, the *Eddie Cantor Show*, and starred as Beulah on both radio and television. She died in 1952. In John Huston's *In This Our Life* (1942), she worries about her son who wants to study law. She is frightened by his ambition, which she sees as unnatural. When, as she had expected, disaster strikes, she cries out: "Ah knew this would happen if he tried to better himself. His place is with us, with the servants; he shouldn't try to make himself better than he is!" So spoke the consciousness of the times—the white man's consciousness.

Butterfly McQueen

Butterfly McQueen's stint as a real-life maid came after her movie career had come to an end. Following her appearance in *Duel in the Sun* (1947), she issued a statement saying she would no longer do "handkerchief head" parts. The series of jobs that followed ranged from taxi dispatcher in New York City to paid companion to a little old lady on Long Island. She received no other movie offers, though she had proved herself to be a talented actress and dancer on the Broadway stage.

Thelma McQueen was born in Tampa, Florida, in 1911, where her father was a stevedore and her mother worked as a domestic. In 1934 she joined Venezuela Jones' Negro Theatre Group in Harlem and soon afterward appeared in a production of *A Midsummer Night's Dream*, dancing in the "Butterfly Ballet." Friends immediately began to call her "Butterfly" and she adopted the name as her own.

She first appeared on Broadway in a review called *Brown Sugar* and a year later in the George Abbott hit, *What a Life*. Turning to movies, she appeared in *Affectionately Yours (1941)*, *Cabin in the Sky* (1943), *I Dood It* (1943), *Since You Went Away* (1944), *Flame of Barbary Coast* (1945), *Mildred Pierce* (1945), and *Duel in the Sun* (1947). But her first

Butterfly McQueen in I Dood It (1943)

movie role remains her most famous: she was twenty-eight years old when she played the squeaky-voiced, frightened slave-child Prissy in *Gone with the Wind* (1939). "Lawsy, Miss Scarlett," she whimpered to Vivien Leigh, "I'se don't know nothin' 'bout birthin' babies."

In 1951 she produced and starred in a one-woman show at Carnegie Hall and in the process lost most of the money she had saved from her Hollywood days. She moved back to Georgia, gave music lessons, appeared on her own radio show, and was then hired as a hostess at the Stone Mountain Memorial, a restoration and museum of Confederate times. Then she returned to the stage to appear in the Broadway musical *The Athenian Touch* (1964) and off-Broadway in *Curley McDimple* (1968).

In 1967, when M-G-M revived *Gone with the Wind*, they asked her to make personal appearances, offering expenses but no salary. Butterfly McQueen refused. She's still turning down "handkerchief head" parts.

Above: Butterfly McQueen in Mildred Pierce (1945)
Below: Gregory Peck and Butterfly McQueen in Duel in the Sun (1947)

In 1939, contralto Marian Anderson was refused permission to sing at Washington's Constitution Hall, which was owned by the Daughters of the American Revolution. Secretary of the Interior Harold Ickes, who had been an NAACP leader in Chicago, suggested she hold her concert on the steps of the Lincoln Memorial. That Easter Sunday Marian Anderson sang to a vast unsegregated audience of seventy-five thousand that stretched a great semicircle around her. She ended her program with "America the Beautiful."

Early on the morning of December 7, 1941, navy messman Dorrie Miller, a tall, broad-shouldered black, was gathering laundry on board the battleship *Arizona* berthed in Pearl Harbor. Suddenly he felt the impact of bombs exploding all around the ship. He rushed to the deck, pulled the wounded captain to safety, took over an unmanned machine gun and shot down at least four enemy planes, becoming one of the first heroes of World War II. Three years later, when he was killed in action aboard the aircraft carrier *Liscome Bay*, Miller was still a messman, though a well-decorated one.

In 1941 the situation in the armed forces was this: the air force and the marines accepted no blacks at all; the navy accepted them only as messmen; and the army accepted only enough to fill vacancies in four all-black units created just after the Civil War. By the end of the war, almost a million blacks had served. For the first time there were black pilots in the air force, black officers in the navy and marines, black women in the WACS and WAVES. Black units were praised as "heroic" by Generals Eisenhower, Mark Clark, and George Patton. Stories of courage and persistence were told about such units as Colonel Benjamin Davis' all-black 99th Pursuit Squadron; the "Red Ball Express," crucial supply line of the entire Normandy invasion; and the 24th Infantry, which had single-handedly won the battle of the New Georgia Islands in the Pacific.

Dr. Charles Drew, a brilliant surgeon, was in charge of organizing and maintaining the American Red Cross Blood Bank; this, despite the fact that as a black he was ineligible to donate his own blood. Due to protests by Dr. Drew and others, blood donations by blacks were accepted by the end of the war, though they were segregated and used only as transfusion for blacks. In 1950 after a serious car accident, Dr. Drew was turned away from a "white" hospital in North Carolina. By the time he was taken to a hospital that would treat him, he had died from loss of blood.

The biggest business of the forties was war. The entire nation threw itself into the business of defense—engaging in the serious game of producing the maximum number of planes, tanks, ships, guns, trucks, and bombs in a minimum of time. It took energy and effort, but Rosie the Riveter's muscle was her badge of honor. Despite the inconvenience of gas rationing and food rationing, she and the few men and boys left at home grew their Victory gardens, saved empty toothpaste tubes and bacon grease, wrapped bandages for the Red Cross, bought war bonds, and participated in the drama of the Common Cause. Big business got bigger; fortunes were made, and the gap widened between rich and poor. War workers in the factories traded their health for cars and refrigerators bought on "time," while their sons did their war work in the muddy foxholes, malarial jungles, and bloody beachheads overseas.

In Hollywood as elsewhere, "patriotism" was the watchword. Movie queens such as Jane Russell, Betty Grable, Rita Hayworth, and Lana Turner posed for pin-up pictures to remind the boys in foxholes what they were fighting for. (All the blacks in the service, it seems, were fighting for the sake of Lena Horne.) The stars appeared at war bond rallies and took their U.S.O. shows to segregated audiences close to the battlefields.

Toward the end of the thirties the movie box office had slumped badly, and even the combination of Bingo, free dish giveaways, and the novelties *The Wizard of Oz* and *Gone with the Wind* were not enough to bring it back to life. But with the beginning of the war and the cycle of war movies, profits again rose. Each of the hundreds of new movies had its complement of evil Germans, bungling Italians, and treacherous Japanese. Each had its American heroes, performing brave deeds and making patriotic speeches in moments of grave personal danger. Americans at home listened to the war news on the radio, then went off to the movies to watch Jimmy Stewart, Tyrone Power, Dana Andrews, Henry Fonda, Clark Gable, and others defend the democracy. The most successful musicals, *Yankee Doodle Dandy* (1942) and *This is the Army* (1943), were full of high-stepping, flag-waving patriotism.

Above left: Leigh Whipper (right) as the battered old stable-buck in Of Mice and Men (1940), one of the first sympathetic portraits of a black in a straight dramatic role. Above right: Kenneth Spencer (center) with members of his platoon in Bataan (1943). Right: Canada Lee and William Bendix in Lifeboat (1944)

Right: The Heaven's General (Kenneth Spencer) (left) and Lucifer Jr. (Rex Ingram) (right) fight for the soul of a napping Little Joe (Eddie ''Rochester'' Anderson).

Below left to right: Georgia Brown (Lena Horne) introduces Little Joe to a life of sin;   Katherine Dunham and her dancers

Cabin in the Sky and Stormy Weather

Taken together, both *Cabin in the Sky* and *Stormy Weather* were a monumental showcase for black musical talent. And both made 1943 the best year Lena Horne was ever to have in the movies. In both films the stories were slight and the music marvelous; in both the wit and energy of the performers elevated the material to a memorable level.

Cabin in the Sky is the story of Little Joe Jackson (Eddie "Rochester" Anderson) and the saving of his soul. On one side stands his good wife Petunia (Ethel Waters) and the Heaven's General (Kenneth Spencer); on the other the gorgeous temptress Georgia Brown (Lena Horne)

Left: On their way to their "Cabin in the Sky," Petunia (Ethel Waters) and Little Joe pause to give thanks as the Heaven's General looks on.   Right: Lena Horne as Selina with Ernest Whitman as Jim Europe, the bandleader

and Lucifer Jr. (Rex Ingram). Lucifer tempts Little Joe with liquor and crap games, a winning sweepstakes ticket, and beautiful Georgia. But goodness prevails in the end and Little Joe and Petunia go off to their "Cabin in the Sky."

The cast included Duke Ellington's Orchestra, Louis Armstrong, John "Bubbles" Sublett, Mantan Moreland, Willie Best, Ruby Dandridge, Butterfly McQueen, Oscar Polk, and the Hall Johnson Choir.

Stormy Weather was meant to be a dramatization of the life of Bill Robinson.

The all-star cast included Cab Calloway and his band, Katherine Dunham and her troupe, Fats Waller, the Nicholas Brothers, Ada Brown, Dooley Wilson, the Tramp Band, the Shadracks, Zuttie Singleton, Mae E. Johnson, Flournoy Miller, Coleman Hawkins, and Taps Miller.

The story is told in the form of flashbacks as Corky (Bill Robinson) reads the twenty-fifth anniversary number of *Theatre World,* which has been dedicated to him. Corky remembers his return from World War I as a member of Jim Europe's famous band. He meets Se-

Below: Fats Waller at the piano as Ada Brown sings out "Basin Street Blues"   Right: A "jungle" number

lina (Lena Horne) at a celebration for the Fifteenth Regiment, and she encourages him to try for a job in a New York theatre as a dancer, but he decides to return to Memphis to work as a dancing waiter at a saloon. When the entire saloon is hired for a Broadway show, Corky comes along. After enough difficulty to make the story interesting, he becomes the star Selina knew he could be. They marry, and the musical numbers go on. They separate, and the musical numbers go on. They are reunited, and there is a grand musical finale.

Left: Bill Robinson backstage with his old army buddy Dooley Wilson (left) and Cab Calloway in zoot suit (right)   Below: Lena Horne and Bill Robinson in one of Stormy Weather's many production numbers

For those with the need to express racist sentiments, the circumstances of the early forties provided a strange paradox. The war with Germany was in opposition to their "master race" philosophy, but if such a philosophy was unacceptable in Europe, how could it be defended in the United States?

As usual, emotion ruled over logic. Although black soldiers were expected to participate in the "democratic struggle," and over a million blacks fought in the war, there was continual trouble at southern training camps and bases, and black soldiers on leave had trouble finding transportation on buses, taxis, or trains. Old Jim Crow was as strong as ever. Yet resistance to it was mounting.

In 1941 a group led by A. Philip Randolph planned a march on Washington with protestors, fifty thousand strong, who meant to demand an end to discrimination. President Roosevelt was moved to act and signed an executive order ending discrimination in defense plants and setting up the Fair Employment Practices Commission. In 1942 the Congress for Racial Equality (CORE) was formed and introduced a nonviolent direct action program, the "sit-in." A year later, rioting broke out

in Detroit, where since the start of the war fifty thousand blacks had come to work in local defense plants. Twenty-five blacks and nine whites were killed; the president declared a state of emergency and sent six thousand soldiers to restore order.

During the years immediately following the war there seemed to come a sort of racial consciousness-raising. In 1947, after trials to discover how "gentlemanly and unflappable" he was, Jackie Robinson was admitted as a player in baseball's major leagues. Twenty years later, when the Los Angeles Dodgers played the Minnesota Twins in the World Series, more than half the players were black.

In 1945 the United Nations was founded, guaranteeing fundamental freedoms to all "without distinction as to race." In 1948 in Charleston, South Carolina, blacks voted for the first time since Reconstruction days, and a year later, Edith Mae Irby was admitted to the University of Arkansas Medical School, marking the first major attempt to integrate colleges in the deep South. In short order, a few black students were enrolled at the University of Tennessee and the University of Louisiana. The decade of tokenism had begun.

Opposite: Following in Stepin Fetchit's footsteps were Mantan Moreland who replaced him in the Charlie Chan series (shown here with Benson Fong as Number One Son and Sydney Toler as Charlie Chan) and . . .   Above: Willie Best in The Arizonian (1935). Etta McDaniels holds him at gunpoint.

Lena Horne

Lena Horne was born in 1917 to one of the "first families" of Brooklyn. Her grandmother was an ardent civil rights worker involved in the early days of the NAACP. Lena's parents were divorced and her mother, an actress, traveled with the Lafayette Players. Her childhood was a patchwork of homes and families—with her grandparents in Brooklyn, her uncle in Georgia, her mother in Atlanta, but most often with strangers. When she was sixteen, she left school to join the chorus of Harlem's Cotton Club, where she worked three shows a night for a salary of twenty-five dollars a week. Though the club was located in the heart of Harlem, few blacks were welcome.

"Don't let customers near you," was the advice she heard over and over from family and friends as she stepped onto the stage wearing just three feathers. She developed the ability to isolate herself from audiences—to become the untouchable woman. Moving back and forth between the black and white worlds, she later described herself as at home in neither.

In 1934 she left the Cotton Club long enough to appear on Broadway in *Dance with Your Gods*, receiving bottom billing as "a quadroon girl." The show closed in a few weeks and she returned to the Cotton Club until she was hired by Noble Sissle to tour with his Society Orchestra. He renamed her Helena Horne with the accent on the "lena" for elegance. Her specialty was an Eleanor Powell-type dance number in which she wore tails and a top hat.

While on tour with the Sissle band, she

Lena Horne and Eddie "Rochester" Anderson in Broadway Rhythm *(1945)*

met and married Louis Jones, intending to retire and be a housewife in Pittsburgh. But the marriage was not a success and she resumed her career, traveling to Hollywood to make *The Duke is Tops*, her first movie, and appearing in the short-lived *Blackbirds of 1939* on Broadway. She then went on tour again as a singer in Charlie Barnett's band. She played the Cafe Society Downtown in New York, then the newly opened Little Trocadero in Hollywood. "Discovered" and signed by M-G-M, she became, in her words, "a butterfly pinned to a column, singing away in Movieland."

In *Panama Hattie* (1942) she did a Latin number in which she danced with the Berry Brothers. Directed by Vincente Minelli, the segment was kept separate from the rest of the film so that southern exhibitors who objected to her appearance could edit it out of the film. In *As Thousands Cheer* (1943), once more she leaned against a pillar and sang. Again, her segment was disposable. She next worked in *Cabin in the Sky* (1943), the musical for which M-G-M had originally signed her. The hostility between Ethel Waters and Lena Horne on the set was to become part of the Hollywood legend.

It was wartime and Lena Horne had become the first black pin-up girl. She toured army camps with the U.S.O. Everywhere she went she played to segregated audiences of soldiers. At Fort Riley, Kansas, after playing to a white audience, she was taken before an audience of black soldiers only to find that the best seats were occupied by a group of German prisoners of war. She walked out.

Hollywood offered too few movie parts to keep her working and she spent the post-war years on the cabaret circuit, of-

Above: Lena Horne in The Ziegfield Follies of 1945   *Below: Lena Horne in* The Dutchess of Idaho *(1950)*

ten subjected to the old humiliations. When she appeared at the Savoy-Plaza hotel in New York, she was given a suite of rooms to dress and rest in, but politely asked to sleep elsewhere. Finally, her contracts with big hotels came to include special clauses guaranteeing her and her musicians the right to use the front door and front elevators, to eat in the hotel's restaurants, to request room service, and to be assured that blacks were welcome in the audience.

In the early fifties she found herself blacklisted from television for several years, due, she believes, to her friendship with Paul Robeson, her work for the Council for African Affairs, and her support of causes which in the McCarthy era were considered questionable.

In 1957 she won her first starring role on Broadway in the Harold Arlen show *Jamaica*.

In 1969, after a thirteen-year absence from the screen, she starred with Richard Widmark in *Death of a Gunfighter*, her first dramatic, nonsinging role.

Observing the civil rights struggle of the sixties, she said in her autobiography, entitled *Lena*, " . . . all of us 'firsts'—first glamour girl, first baseball player, first this-that-and-the-other—had reached the end of our usefulness . . . . We were sops, tokens, buy-offs for the white race's conscience. Now millions of Negro people are reaching out as a mass to take what has long been denied them."

Her autobiography begins with this quotation from Mari Evans:
"If there be sorrow
let it be
for things undone
. . .
        unrealized
unattained."

In her first dramatic role, Lena Horne marries Richard Widmark in Death of a Gunfighter *(1969).*

Ethel Waters

"No performer was ever pulled up out of a childhood so dark and cold," Ethel Waters once wrote. She was born in the slums of Chester, Pennsylvania, in 1900 and raised by her grandmother. By the time she was fourteen, she was married, separated, and earning fourteen dollars a week as a hotel chambermaid. Her highest ambition was to be a ladies' maid to an actress.

On her seventeenth birthday, at a Halloween party in a Philadelphia saloon, she stood up and sang "When You're a Long Way from Home." Two vaudevillians offered her ten dollars a week to join their act. Billed as "Sweet Mama Stringbean—direct from St. Louis" she preceded their act and sang "St. Louis Blues." The audience adored her.

Discovering the vaudevillians had been pocketing part of her earnings every week, she left them, joined the Hills Sisters, and played small-time vaudeville all over the country. In Atlanta, she appeared on the same bill as Bessie Smith. At the end of a year's tour, she played the Howard in Washington, a black-owned theatre where three times a week only "light-skinned colored folk" could attend performances.

Convinced she could never make a living in show business, she returned to Philadelphia and took a job at the Auto-

Top: Jeanette McDonald and Ethel Waters in Cairo (1942)   Right: Ethel Waters in StageDoor Canteen (1943)

mat. But friends convinced her to work part time in a local saloon, and it was there that she added "the shimmy shake" to her act. Soon she was offered a week's work in Harlem vaudeville and then booked into Edmund's Cellar, which she called "the last stop on the way down in show business." Black Swan Record Company hired her, and to promote her records "Down Home Blues" and "There'll be Some Changes Made" she toured with Fletcher Henderson's Black Swan Jazz Masters.

Over and over again, Ethel Waters refused to play white vaudeville—"the white time"—fearing that audiences wouldn't understand her work. But a friend named Earl Dancer, who later joined her act and even later produced her first Broadway show, convinced her to try. She auditioned in Chicago and found herself on the Keith circuit—the white bigtime. Then in 1927 she opened in her first Broadway musical, *Africana*. In her autobiography she related that King Vidor sent a talent man east to offer her a part in *Hallelujah*, but "he was stalled on the job by colored theatrical people unfriendly to me." Soon afterward, another Hollywood offer came through and she appeared in *On with the Show* (1929), her first movie, singing "Am I Blue!"

By 1939 Ethel Waters was the highest-paid woman performer on Broadway. That year she played her first dramatic role, in *Mamba's Daughters*. It was more than a play to her; it was the story of her family's life. Mamba, with her fierce primitive religion and her losing struggle against a white man's world, reminded her of her own mother.

Returning to Hollywood, she appeared in *Cairo* (1940), *Tales of Manhattan* (1942), and *Cabin in the Sky* (1943). About *Cabin* she wrote, "I won all my battles on that picture. But like many other performers, I was to discover that winning arguments in Hollywood is costly. Six years were to pass before I could get another movie job." All offers—movie, night club, or theatre—stopped coming in. She had trouble with Internal Revenue. She was swamped with debts and unpaid bills. "Retiring" to the basement of a friend's house on 149th Street in Harlem, she hardly ever went out, ashamed of being a has-been.

Finally she was contacted by Twentieth-Century Fox and asked to test for a part in a John Ford film. She went to California and made the test, feeling that her entire career depended on the results. The movie was *Pinky* (1949), her performance brought her an Oscar nomination, and the bad years seemed over. She opened on Broadway in *The Member of the Wedding* in 1950, repeated the role in the 1952 film and was again nominated for the Academy Award. She played television's first Beulah during the 1950 season and appeared in *The Heart is a Rebel* (1956) and *The Sound and the Fury* (1959).

The woman who popularized the songs "Heat Wave," "Dinah," and "Supper Time," who helped raise more than twenty children, none her own, who gave much of her money to charity, published a best-selling autobiography in 1951. Near the end of *His Eye Is on the Sparrow*, she wrote, "And now I have told it all, and it has been an ache and a joy both to look over this big shoulder of mine at all my yesterdays. And there are no regrets, not even sighs, only joy and thanksgiving to the Lord for this life He gave me."

Opposite above: *Julie Harris and Ethel Waters in* The Member of the Wedding *(1952)*
Opposite below: *Joanne Woodward, Ethel Waters, and Yul Brynner in* The Sound and the Fury *(1959)*

The Racial Injustice Films: Home of the Brave, Pinky, Lost Boundaries, Intruder in the Dust

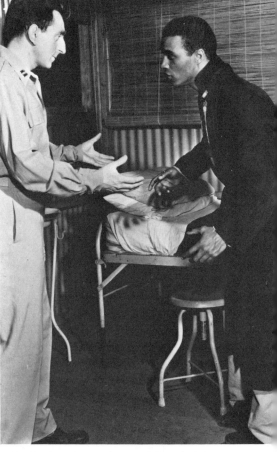

Left: Lloyd Bridges and James Edwards in Home of the Brave (1949)   Right: After Bridges death, Edwards is paralyzed. Jeff Corey, as a psychiatrist, helps him walk.

In Hollywood, 1949 was the year of the social statement. In a burst of energy known as a film "cycle," the year produced *Home of the Brave, Pinky, Lost Boundaries,* and *Intruder in the Dust.* Though all were well intentioned and even courageous for their time, they also demonstrated the social evasions of the time. None except *Intruder in the Dust* dealt with the issues in a straightforward manner. All spoke of "tolerance." No past history was considered, and few questions were posed about the social structure underlying racism. And the problem of "passing for white," the principle consideration of *Pinky* and *Lost Boundaries,* was not very relevant to the majority of blacks.

In *Home of the Brave,* the likeable Private Moss cracks up as a result of the death of his best friend and repeated racial harassment by men in his platoon. Encouraged by a sympathetic psychiatrist, he voices his emotions, finally crying, "if you're colored, you stink," then recovers, finds another white friend, and together they go off toward a happy ending. The problem is raised, but the optimistic ending is at best simplistic.

The black community hospital in *Lost Boundaries* rejects a hopeful young doctor because he is "too light," and the doctor decides to "pass." He does so successfully for twenty years, but he is ultimately discovered and rejected by the white community he lives in. So a local minister preaches a sermon on "tolerance" and the community repents, at least in part.

Jeanne Crain, who plays a nurse in *Pinky,* has two alternatives—to "pass" in the North or to return to her home in the South and accept a life much like that of her washerwoman grandmother, Aunt Dicey. Only through the intervention of a

Above: Mel Ferrar and Beatrice Pearson marry in Lost Boundaries (1959)   Below: Years later. The Carters have raised a family and successfully passed for white, but their tranquility is disturbed when the townspeople learn they are black.

Right: Aunt Dicey (Ethel Waters) and Pinky
(Jeanne Crain)   Below: Frederick O'Neal and
Nina Mae McKinney (right) are checked out by
local police as Pinky (Jeanne Crain) looks on in
Pinky (1949).

crusty old white lady with a conscience and an estate and a lawyer who respects the old lady's dying wishes does Pinky win anything like equal rights and a bright future. The implication is clear: the "rights" remain in the hands of the small-town whites to give over or deny.

In both of these films the roles of blacks were played by whites. Thus Hollywood was able to include an interracial love scene in *Pinky* (because it really was not), and to enlist greater sympathy from the white moviegoers, who were better able to relate to the dilemma posed.

Intruder in the Dust, the last of the cycle and perhaps the most honest, introduced Juano Hernandez, who played a proud, strong, black man, hated by a racist southern town, and falsely accused of murder. Although he is saved through the efforts of an old lady and a young boy, both white, he realizes, along with the audience, that it was largely luck, and that a black man has little chance of receiving equal treatment before the law. As a man, Hernandez is reminiscent of Robeson; as a performer, he brought his great talent to all the roles he played. But never did the parts measure up to the stature of the man.

Juano Hernandez receives the stares of his "neighbors" in Intruder in the Dust *(1949).*

School desegregation represented the major civil rights thrust of the fifties, a period in the nation's history which combined apathy, fear, and prosperity in interesting proportions. The deadly specter of the atom bomb overhung the decade. Thousands of families rushed to build underground bomb shelters, which they vowed to protect from intruders with their lives.

Communists had fought the Japanese in China and Korea and in China had gone on to defeat the U.S.-supported government of Chiang Kai-shek. Inspired by the successful Chinese Revolution of 1949, and unwilling the next year to see the Japanese occupation replaced by an American one in the South, Korean Communists, equipped with Russian arms, determined to fight. American response was called a "police action" designed to "contain" communism and, later, "to go to the brink of war" to combat it. Joseph McCarthy, a senator with a taste of power and questionable scruples, built himself an empire of fear which capitalized on the "growing red menace."

Forgetting McCarthy and Korea as soon as it could, the nation that "liked Ike" continued to grow. Suburbia was born and along with it the commuter life style, the Saturday night cocktail party, the Sunday barbeque, the station wagon, the super highway, and the shopping center. It was a time of hula hoops and Davy Crockett hats and pop-it beads. And a time for strange, new groups to be born—urban teenage gangs, who called themselves "Lords" and "Kings," who carried switchblade knives and defended their "turf"; Hell's Angels, roving motorcycle gangs who carried chains and dressed in black leather; and Beatniks, restless, alienated, disenchanted yet passionate, a counter culture expressed in the writings of Jack Kerouac, Gregory Corso, Allen Ginsberg. And just as the forties had created the bobby soxers and "Sinatramania," so the fifties created rock hysteria and the Elvis Presley twitch.

And then there was television. In 1950 Americans were buying 100,000 television sets a week. From the early days of Milton Berle or wrestling or nothing at all, television grew to the point where the average family watched it for nearly fifty hours a week. Along with Berle, Arthur Godfrey, Lucille Ball, and Sid Caesar brought their special qualities to the screen, live drama came into the living room courtesy of the U.S. Steel Hour or Kraft Television Theatre, situation comedies such as *Mr. Peepers* and *Leave It to Beaver* entertained us lightly, and public affairs programming of Ed Murrow and Huntley/Brinkley informed us heavily. There were cop shows (Sergeant Friday and his matter-of-fact *Dragnet*), quiz shows (Charles van Doren and his ill-gotten $129,000 on *Twenty-one*), and specials (Mary Martin flying across the screen in *Peter Pan*). There were social satirists such as Mort Sahl, Shelly Berman, Nichols and May, and the controversial Lenny Bruce.

The movies gave us the old reliable detective and Western fare of Kirk Douglas and Gary Cooper with what now appear to be moderate doses of sex and violence; the high-society films of Grace Kelly; the new-born social rebellion expressed by Marlon Brando and James Dean; the comedy of Dean Martin and Jerry Lewis; the musicals of Gene Kelly and the ageless Fred Astaire; science fiction, inspired by a growing technology; and the "art film" imported from Europe.

During the middle fifties the romantic "lost cause" movies of slavery days in the South gave way to the intense, cynical view of Tennessee Williams. Westerns began to treat the Indian with some measure of sympathy, and blacks began to be seen as symbolic of the struggle against oppression.

Sidney Poitier

"It has been a long journey to this moment." In April 1964, as Sidney Poitier accepted the Academy Award for his performance in *Lilies of the Field,* he spoke those quiet words. And for all who listened, the full meaning of his words was clear.

Sidney Poitier's parents were tomato farmers who sailed from their home on Cat Island in the Bahamas to Miami twice a year to market their crops. In February 1927, during one of those trips, Sidney, the youngest of their children, was born. Cat Island was a primitive place. There were no roads, no cars, no electricity, no schools. Poitier's parents were poor, as were all those who lived on the island. He describes his childhood as free and secure.

When he was eleven, the family moved to Nassau and enrolled Sidney in school. Eighteen months later, he had finished with it, deciding to learn a trade instead. But the only work he could find was ditch digging for two dollars a day. Moving to Miami, he worked as a delivery boy, parking lot attendant, and sanitation man before he decided to try New York. He describes himself as arriving in New York, not yet seventeen, completely alone, and with a dollar and a half in his pocket. He washed dishes and plucked

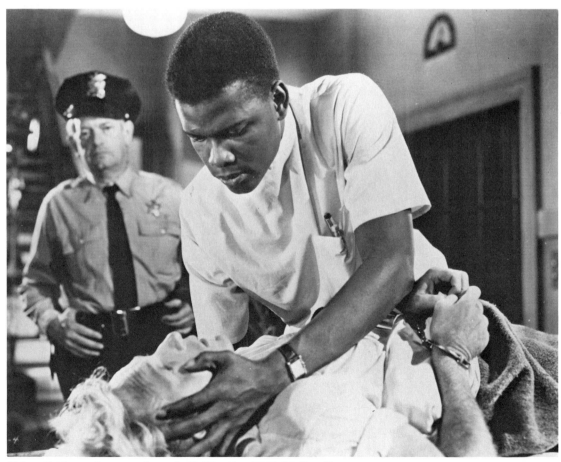

Sidney Poitier as the young doctor in No Way Out *(1950), his first film.*

chickens for the Waldorf Astoria kitchens, slept in the men's room at the Greyhound bus station, or in warm weather on the roof of a midtown office building.

Back in New York after a year in the army, he read an ad in the *Amsterdam News:* "ACTORS WANTED." The American Negro Theatre was holding auditions. Actor Frederick O'Neal listened to Poitier read in his halting West Indian patois, then threw him out, saying, "Don't waste our time. You're no actor and you can't ever be one." So he bought a radio, magazines, and newspapers and, after finishing a day's work in the garment district, spent hours learning to read and speak well enough to audition again. Six months later he did, and was accepted as a trainee; his classmates were Harry Belafonte, Ossie Davis, and Ruby Dee. Studying intensely, Poitier began to appear in the theatre's weekly productions. A Broadway director offered him a small part in an all-black production of *Lysistrata,* then another as male understudy in the Broadway revival of *Anna Lucasta.*

In 1950 Poitier appeared in *No Way Out,* his first movie. The reviewers were impressed. His next part, in *Cry, the Beloved Country,* was to be filmed on location in South Africa. Since blacks were not allowed to enter the country except as servants to a white man, Poitier and others in the cast signed an agreement stating that they were "indentured servants" to producer Zoltan Korda. His next important role was that of the student Gregory Miller in the film version of the Evan Hunter novel *Blackboard Jungle* (1955). In 1957, his performance in *Edge of the City* brought him an Oscar nomination.

He was now an established star—the first black to reach that point, not as an

Sidney Poitier and Tony Curtis in The Defiant Ones *(1958)*

entertainer or comedian but as a dramatic actor. By demonstrating a kind of personal superiority, he had become a symbol of the black who could "make it" in white America. Those who took pride in the fact that Poitier was "in" ignored the standards set by whites for letting him in. To be considered human, he had to be no less than perfect. And he was willing to try.

Militants cried out for equal standards. Not until 1964 were their sentiments aptly expressed in the film title *Nothing But a Man*. And Poitier was not in that movie, but perhaps by continuing to be super-Sidney, he had made it possible.

In *Lilies of the Field* (1963), he was goodness personified. And his reward was an Oscar. In *In the Heat of the Night* (1967), in which a black detective wins the respect of a redneck southern sheriff; *To Sir with Love* (1967), in which a black teacher wins the respect of rowdy teenage students; *Guess Who's Coming to Dinner* (1967), in which a black scientist, a Nobel prize candidate, wins the right to marry a rich white girl; and finally in the 1971 film *Brother John*, in which he plays a kind of mystical messenger from God, Poitier continued to play the-man-who-could-win-because-he-was-perfect.

Curiously, just one year before, his friend Harry Belafonte was the angel in *The Angel Levine*. By 1972 both of them seemed to have had enough of portraying deities. They appeared together in *Buck and the Preacher* as nothing but men, heroic but nevertheless human. Placing them in the context of their times, both were heroes of the age of integration. Both earned millions of dollars in show business. Both helped push wide the door for blacks in American films. And both are now fighting to be "relevant" as well as rich.

Lilies of the Field (1963) brought Poitier an Oscar.

Sidney Poitier and Rod Steiger in *In the Heat of the Night* (1967)

Dorothy Dandridge

In an interview in the early 1950s Dorothy Dandridge said, "No producers are knocking at my door. There just aren't that many parts for Negro actresses."

Hearing that Otto Preminger planned to film *Carmen Jones*, she went on a one-woman campaign for the leading role. She phoned Preminger. He told her the part was too small for her, thinking she wanted to play sweet little Cindy Lou, who loses Joe to Carmen. He alternately argued that she was "too sweet" or "too regal" to be Carmen. She replied, "I can play Carmen or a nun and audiences will believe either role."

Preminger agreed to let her read for the part, and she showed up wearing tight-fitting capri pants and an off-the-shoulder blouse. She got the part. "But I was only acting," she told an interviewer. "It's not me."

What she really was remains a mystery to those who have watched her films. She could have chosen to remain the "darling of café society," continuing to play all the smart supper clubs, such as La Vie en Rose, Ciro's, Mocambo, and the Cafe de Paris in London. She was, in fact, the first black to play the Empire Room at the Waldorf Astoria. Or she could have continued to play the few "singing mulatto" roles that came along, such as Carmen, for which she won an Academy Award nomination, and *Porgy and Bess*, in which she played Bess in 1959. But she dreamed of being a Helen Hayes. And that too might have been possible.

Dorothy Dandridge was born in Cleveland in 1924, the daughter of a minister and an actress. Her parents separated, and with her mother Ruby directing, Dorothy and her sister Vivian became "The Wonder Children," a singing and dancing act. They settled in Los Angeles, where Ruby hoped all three could get movie work. While they waited, she gave dancing lessons to support them. She later became well-known as a regular on the *Beulah* show on radio and television.

When Dorothy was thirteen, she appeared in a bit part in the Marx Brothers classic *A Day at the Races*. At fifteen,

she, Vivian, and a friend joined Jimmy Lunceford's band as a singing trio. She worked as a chorus girl and later as a singer in night clubs, then married Harold Nicholas, one of the dancing Nicholas Brothers.

Four years later, she was divorced and back in show business as a singer at Hollywood's Mocambo. She had a few small parts in movies during the forties, including *Lady From Louisiana* (1941), *Drums of the Congo* (1942), and *Hit Parade of 1943*. But it was as a night-club torch singer that she made her reputation, until in 1953 she was cast as the demure school teacher in *Bright Road* and a year later as the memorable Carmen in *Carmen Jones*.

After *Porgy and Bess*, the movie offers came few and far between and in the sixties Dorothy Dandridge's private troubles became public knowledge. Hollywood friends had convinced her to invest $150,000 in the Arizona oil fields. Later, she put more and more money into the oil investment and ultimately lost it all. A newspaper report states: "On the same day in 1962 when she divorced her second husband, Jack Dennison, she had her house foreclosed and her mentally retarded daughter left on her doorstep by the private hospital which had been caring for her." A year later she filed for bankruptcy, although her income for the previous two years had topped $100,000.

Her last film, *Malaga*, was made in England in 1962. Three years later, just after she had returned from a vacation in Mexico and days before she was scheduled to open at Basin Street East in New York, Dorothy Dandridge was found dead in her apartment in Hollywood. The coroner's report: overdose of drugs used to treat depression.

Above: John Justin and Dorothy Dandridge in Island in the Sun (1957)   Below: Dorothy Dandridge as a native girl in Tamango (1959)

Harry Belafonte

"From the top of his head right down the white shirt, he's the most beautiful man I ever set eyes on," Diahann Carroll said of Harry Belafonte. He is also powerful, commanding, and talented, with a sweet husky voice that can captivate a stadium full of people. Belafonte is a millionaire, has made over a dozen best-selling records, half a dozen films, starred on Broadway, and hosted the *Tonight Show* on CBS television. He has been called the "Calypso King" and the "First Negro Matinee Idol." How does Harry Belafonte go about proving he is also a "man of the people"?

He puts on ragged clothes, grows a scraggly beard and moustache, blackens his teeth, takes to chewing tobacco, becomes the boozy, bleary-eyed, gun-toting preacher of the High and Low Order of the Holiness Persuasion Church in *Buck and the Preacher* (1972) and proves himself an actor of great merit.

In the early 1950s Harold George Belafonte Jr.'s star rose straight to the sky. Before that, he had looked for work as a dramatic actor and found none; he had tried a career as a pop singer and rejected it. But as a folk balladeer, he found almost overnight success and a medium he could respect.

He was born in 1927, within ten days of Sidney Poitier, the man who was to become his best friend. There are striking similarities in the backgrounds of the two men. Although Belafonte was born in Harlem and Poitier in the Bahamas, Belafonte spent much of his youth in Jamaica. Both came from poor families, although Belafonte's childhood in Harlem on Home Relief, often cold and hungry, may have been the less tolerable. His mother worked as a domestic and sometimes a dressmaker. His father, a merchant seaman, was rarely at home. When he was

Harry Belafonte and Dorothy Dandridge in Bright Road (1953)

Left: Belafonte serenades a store dummy in The World, the Flesh and the Devil *(1959)*
Right: Belafonte in Odds Against Tomorrow *(1959)*

nine years old, his mother took him to Jamaica, where he lived with relatives or boarded out at several different schools until he was thirteen. He came back to New York, attended high school for a few years, got his working papers, and dropped out.

In 1944 he joined the navy for a two-year tour of duty, then worked as a maintenance man in a New York City apartment building. A tenant gave him a ticket to an American Negro Theatre production. Belafonte was so intrigued he offered to work as a volunteer stagehand and later as an actor. There he met Poitier and the two became good friends. "We'd split unemployment checks and theatre tickets," Belafonte later said. "Sometimes, when we could wangle only one ticket, we'd take turns. One of us would see the first act, come out with the stub and a synopsis, the other would go in for the second act and so on."

Then came two years of touring as a pop singer, at which he was moderately successful but reportedly unhappy, followed by a year when he owned a restaurant in Greenwich Village called The Sage. During that time, his interest in folk music, vaguely remembered from his days in Jamaica, was rekindled. With the help of a manager, he began to study folk songs; he put together an act and was booked into New York's Village Vanguard. His success was instantaneous and he went from there to the elegant uptown Blue Angel. In quick succession he had a recording contract, a booking in a Las Vegas club, and a movie offer. In *Bright Road* (1953) he played a school principal, in love with a demure Dorothy Dandridge. He later called the film "a bland Lassie-like thing."

After being booked into the Thunderbird hotel, he arrived in Las Vegas and found that all black entertainers stayed at one of a few rickety boarding houses at the edge of town. In subsequent years he was permitted to stay at the hotal where he was working and to eat in the dining room. Finally in 1955, he and two friends "integrated" the swimming pool and the game rooms. That same year, while waiting to go on stage at Chicago's Palmer House, he was approached by the maitre d' hotel who had recognized his color but not his identity and told him to leave. Belafonte left.

A Broadway appearance in John Murray Anderson's *Almanac* (1953), singing "Hold 'Em Joe," "Acorn in the Meadow," and "Mark Twain," won Belafonte a Tony award as Best Supporting Actor of the year, and in 1954 his first LP album, *Mark Twain and Other Favorites*, was released. Otto Preminger, who had seen him in *Almanac*, signed him to play Joe in the film *Carmen Jones*.

In 1957, he appeared in *Island in the Sun* with Joan Fontaine. The two were hardly permitted to touch one another in the film; even so, a bill was introduced in the South Carolina legislature proposing to levy a fine of $5,000 on any theatre that exhibited it. Producer Daryl Zanuck announced he would personally pay any fines, and the bill never passed. Then in 1959, his own newly formed Harbel Productions released *The World, the Flesh, and the Devil*, in which Belafonte played one of three survivors of an atomic war, and *Odds Against Tomorrow*, which cast him as a jazz musician turned criminal. While filming *The Angel Levine* (1970), a member of his apprentice film crew brought him a script to read. It was *Buck and the Preacher*. And Belafonte, the corporate entity, star, beautiful person, became the Preacher, man of the people.

Belafonte plays the preacher in Buck and the Preacher *(1972).*

Arthur Kennedy and James Edwards, blinded war veterans who are friends until Kennedy discovers Edwards is black in Bright Victory *(1951).*

Carmen Jones

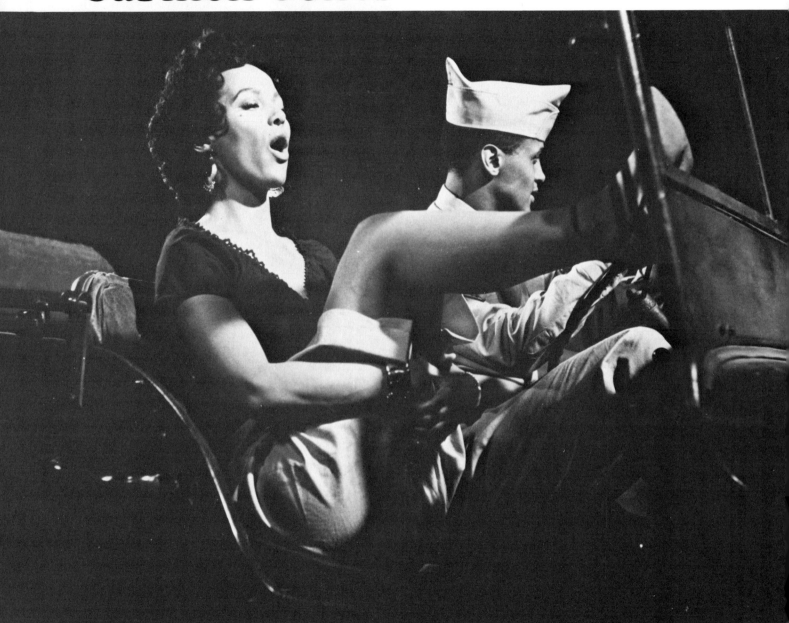

Carmen and Joe at the beginning

During the filming of *Carmen Jones*, the wise-cracking Pearl Bailey remarked, "I'll bet this is the first time Bizet has ever been dr-aw-l-ed!"

The music is the familiar Bizet "Carmen" and the modern lyrics are more often jarring than compatible with it. The voices of both Carmen and Joe were dubbed, Carmen being sung by the soprano Marilyn Horne and Joe by Le Vern Hutcherson, who starred in the national company of *Porgy and Bess*.

But if the combination sometimes seemed strange, the audience drowned in the whirlwind energy of the lavish all-black musical, was given little time to think about it. The film is set in the United States during World War II. Dorothy Dandridge is Carmen, who works in a parachute factory, and Harry Belafonte is Joe, the solider who deserts from the army for her. Joe and Carmen run away to Chicago. Though Carmen loves him, she is drawn to the powerful prizefighter, Husky Miller (Joe Adams), who is determined to win her. Carmen and Joe quarrel, and she leaves him. He goes after her and, in desperation, strangles her.

Featured as Carmen's good-time friends are Pearl Bailey and Diahann Carroll. Olga James plays the good little girl who loses Joe to Carmen and Brock Peters the snarling, scheming sergeant. Carmen's grandmother is played by Madame Sul Te Wan, who was said to have made her first film appearance in *The Birth of a Nation*.

Husky Miller (Joe Adams), the prizefighter who falls in love with Carmen

Above: "De nine of Spades—dat ole boy!" Diahann Carroll and Pearl Bailey watch as Carmen turns over the death card.   Below: Carmen and Joe at the end—as the cards predicted!

Sammy Davis

Behind bars in Convicts 4 *(1962)*

A man who worked with Sammy Davis in the early sixties wrote this about him: "Sam has more friends than any other performer I can think of. People love this guy. But he carries on as though he's an orphan. I'm sure in Sammy's mind, he still thinks of himself as the kid in the army, the one who got stomped on, spat upon and beaten. Sam is out to win every bigot in the world. For every nine he wins over, it's the one who got away that bugs him."

In his autobiography *Yes I Can*, Sammy Davis described himself. "I had a mental picture of the whole world split in half, with me standing in the middle, the Negroes on one side glaring at me and the whites on the other side, laughing. What do I have to accomplish before I can walk on both sides of the world in peace? With dignity?"

It is the incredible energy of the man that is so amazing. Like a lightbulb with its own nuclear power plant. He explained it as trying to "dance down the barriers" between himself and other people. "My talent was the weapon, the power, the way for me to fight. It was the one way I might hope to affect a man's thinking."

For Sammy Davis, home was a railroad flat on the corner of 140th Street and Amsterdam Avenue in Harlem where, he recalls, "the back windows were always kept shut to keep out the smell of the garbage people threw out their windows."

Davis in Sergeants 3 (1962)

But it was only a place to come back to between gigs. He was born in 1925. His parents, both vaudeville dancers, soon separated, and he was on the road with his father before he was three. Sammy Davis spent hundreds of hours watching his father and his "uncle," Will Mastin, do what he later described as "fast and furious flash dancing . . . with fifteen minutes to make an impression or starve." Sammy watched, learned, and joined the act before he was four. By the time he was eight he was getting feature billing, and by the time he was fifteen "The Will Mastin Trio and Sammy Davis Jr." had "crossed the country twenty-three times and played so much time in Canada we were considered residents of Montreal."

After a stint in the army, he returned to the act. "After the war, I was so hungry, I was trying to do everything. I could do fifty impersonations. Play the drums. Play the trumpet. Play the bass fiddle. Play the piano. Dance. Sing. Tell jokes."

The act got better and better bookings— a tour of the RKO circuit with Mickey Rooney; the Capitol Theater in New York with Frank Sinatra; Slapsie Maxie's in Los Angeles; and finally in 1951, Ciro's in Hollywood. They were into the top-drawer night club circuit—New York, Chicago, Hollywood, Miami, Las Vegas— and Davis did guest spots on television, singing, quipping, impersonating, then dropping in a few chords on the piano, a few licks on the vibes or a horn—all

guaranteed crowd pleasers. They had made the big time and the big money. As Sammy Davis told it: "I bought twelve suits at a time, $175 a whack. I bought tailor-made shirts, cars—fast ones. I bought gold cigarette cases for everybody. All my life I wanted to buy something in a store and not ask how much. I had credit everywhere. Between 1951 and 1954 I must have blown $150,000."

Then on the way from Las Vegas to California in 1954 Davis's car collided with another car. He lost an eye and it seemed to him that his whole career was blown. But just months later, he opened again at Ciro's in Hollywood. It was the same intense, driving, exciting Sammy Davis— or maybe an even more determined Sammy Davis with an eye patch.

His first film was *The Benny Goodman Story* and his first Broadway show was *Mr. Wonderful.* Both opened in 1956. In the next few years he made over thirty records, appeared in a dozen movies, played hundreds of club dates and hundreds of benefits. In 1964 he starred in *Golden Boy* on Broadway and in 1968 took it to London.

Davis was definitely on top. In 1944 he could not get a room in a Las Vegas hotel, although he was performing there. Less than twenty years later, he put nearly a million dollars on the line and bought part interest in a neighboring hotel. He owns a vast house in Beverly Hills and another in Palm Springs, drives three of the world's most expensive cars—in short, he lives like the millionaire that he is. He has tried as many life styles as he has dance steps. As a member of Frank Sinatra's rat pack, as a black militant, as a "one-eyed Jewish Negro," as a Kennedy Democrat converted to a Nixon Republican, Sammy Davis just keeps on trying.

Davis in One More Time (1970)

Diahann Carroll

Diahann Carroll in Carmen Jones *(1954), her first film*

The tall, slim girl in the écru taffeta knickers stands in the spotlight, smiling sweetly, her eyes brilliant, reaching out with graceful, expressive hands, wrapping herself and her audience in song. Diahann Carroll. She once told an interviewer, "An audience is like a strange child, a child I don't know. I mean a baby sitting there in the darkness and it's up to me to win them."

From her first appearance on *Chance of a Lifetime*, a television talent show in the early fifties, Diahann Carroll has displayed a regal quality and great sense of style. She won top honors for three weeks running and earned $3,000. With that nest egg, she convinced her parents to allow her to leave college and try show business.

Lou Walters booked her into the Latin Quarter for a week. As she tells it, "I sang every number in an entirely different key from the orchestra. I was in a state of shock." Still, someone must have liked her. Her engagement was extended to four weeks, and she was signed to appear on Broadway in *House of Flowers* (1954) as Ottilie, the innocent virgin in the bordello. Although the show was

Paul Newman, Joanne Woodward, Diahann Carroll, and Sidney Poitier in Paris Blues *(1961)*

short lived, her performance brought her to the attention of the critics—and to Richard Rodgers, who decided he would like one day to write a show for her. Her first movie appearance was in *Carmen Jones* (1954). Then came television appearances, including the first on the *Jack Paar Show,* where she later appeared more than fifty times. She played in *Porgy and Bess* in 1959, then *Paris Blues* (1961) with Sidney Poitier. She also appeared briefly in *Goodbye Again,* which was being shot in Paris at the same time.

In 1962 Richard Rodgers made good his promise to star her in a show. She opened in *No Strings* to glowing reviews. About the show she said, "I felt it was time for people to enter the theatre, watch a Negro perform for two-and-a-half hours as an actor and leave saying, 'I'll be doggoned. You know that girl stood there and was just like anybody else.' " The "just like anybody else" she was describing is Barbara Woodruff, *Vogue's* top fashion model in Paris who falls in love with a Pulitzer-prize-winning novelist and in many ways not unlike the real Diahann Carroll.

She was born in the Bronx in 1935. Her father was a subway conductor; her mother a nurse. When she was ten years old, she won a Metropolitan Opera scholarship which she gave up almost immediately because it interfered with her roller skating. She went to the High School of Music and Art and worked as a model after school, then enrolled in N.Y.U., intending to major in sociology. Her success on *Chance of a Lifetime* helped her convince her family that show business might be a better career than sociology.

She has played most of the top supper club circuit. In 1967 she appeared at the Persian Room of the Plaza hotel in New York and in clubs in Miami Beach, California and Las Vegas, starred in television specials with Maurice Chevalier and Harry Belafonte, appeared on the Danny Kaye and Ed Sullivan shows, and starred in the movie *Hurry Sundown.* The next year she become the star of her own television series, *Julia,* in which she played a widowed nurse with a six-year-old son.

In one of the early shows, Julia telephones a doctor to apply for a job.

"I'm colored," she says.

"What color are you?" he asks.

"A Negro."

"Were you always Negro or are you just trying to be fashionable?"

Diahann Carroll with Jim Brown in The Split (1968)

Eight-year-old Linda Carol Brown lived in Topeka, Kansas. Every day since beginning school she had taken the long and dangerous walk through a railroad yard to catch a bus which would carry her to the McKinley School, twenty-one blocks away, despite the fact that there was an elementary school within just five blocks of her home. Linda Brown could not attend that school. Kansas law allowed communities to set up separate schools for black students and white students. In 1951, with the assistance of the NAACP, Linda's father took the case to court. The federal district court in Kansas ruled against them and the decision was appealed to the Supreme Court. In 1953 the Supreme Court agreed to hear the case, known as *Brown v. Topeka Board of Education*. On Monday, May 17, 1954, the decision was handed down in favor of the Browns; "separate but equal" was no longer the law of the land. Segregationists called it Black Monday.

A year earlier, the editor of the Richmond *Times* had written, "School segregation is the keystone in the arch and if knocked out, the whole segregated structure will collapse." In fact, legal inroads had already been made: in three historic NAACP suits in 1950 it was held that Jim Crow was illegal on interstate dining cars (*Henderson v. United States*); equal education required more than equal buildings (*Sweatt v. Painter*); and schools could not segregate black students from whites once they had been admitted to previously all-white schools (*McLaurin v. Oklahoma State Regents*). By the middle of the 1950s the NAACP had 1,500 chapters and nearly 400,000 members; it won forty-three of the forty-seven suits it took to the Supreme Court between 1941 and 1963.

The first important test of *Brown v. Topeka Board of Education* came in 1957 when Governor Orval Faubus of Arkansas defied a federal court order to admit nine black pupils to Little Rock High School and called out the National Guard to prevent their entry. Later that same month President Eisenhower ordered 1,000 federal troops to protect the students as they entered the school, and Governor Faubus countered by closing all Little Rock schools. When they were reopened a year later at the insistence of the board of education, blacks were in attendance at several "white" schools.

In 1955 a fourteen-year-old boy from Chicago named Emmett Till was vacationing with relatives in Mississippi. He was said to have whistled at a white woman in a country store. "To teach him a lesson," Till was beaten, shot in the head, tied to a cotton gin wheel, and finally dumped into the Tallahatchie River. Two white men were accused, tried, and acquitted.

In December of the same year a weary, middle-aged seamstress named Rosa Parks refused to give up her seat on a Montgomery, Alabama, bus to a white man. She was arrested. This single event sparked the Montgomery bus boycott, the rise of the leadership of Dr. Martin Luther King, and the policy of nonviolent resistance.

For more than a year Montgomery blacks refused to ride the buses until, in 1956, the Supreme Court ruled bus segregation unconstitutional. This victory inspired the creation of the Southern Christian Leadership Conference, headed at first by the Reverend King and staffed with young black ministers and laymen trained for political action. The next year Congress passed the first civil rights bill since 1875, which although ineffective, recognized the need for legislation and provided legal avenues for the protection of civil rights.

Together with the *Brown v. Topeka Board of Education* decision in 1954, the Montgomery action sparked a decade of intensified civil rights activity; the drive for school desegregation had become an explosive demand for full and equal rights.

Former football star Woody Strode (left) with Jeffrey Hunter and Constance Towers in John Ford's Sergeant Rutledge (1960). Strode played a strong heroic black man.

Porgy and Bess

No one except Samuel Goldwyn and Sammy Davis seemed to want to make a movie out of *Porgy and Bess* in 1959. The seventy-six year old Goldwyn wanted it badly enough to spend $7 million to do it, and Sammy Davis wanted it enough to go on a one-man campaign for the part of Sportin' Life.

Harry Belafonte turned down the part of Porgy. As a black man in 1959, he must have felt there was something wrong with Porgy standing up and singing, "I got plenty of nothin' and nothin's plenty for me." Civil rights groups applauded his decision and urged Goldwyn to drop the project. Even Sidney Poitier, who eventually signed to play the lead, was reluctant. But after Poitier was persuaded, Goldwyn was quickly able to assemble the rest of the cast. Even a huge fire which destroyed the sets and costumes and caused $2.5 million in damages hardly slowed him down.

The story, as written by Du Bose Heyward, is set on the Charleston wharf known as Catfish Row early in the twentieth century. The beautiful Bess (Doro-

Clara (Diahann Carroll) holds her baby and sings "Summertime."

128

thy Dandridge) comes to town with the brutish Crown (Brock Peters). Crown kills a local man during a crap game and runs away.

All of Catfish Row turns against Bess, except for Porgy, a cripple, who takes her in. They fall in love. Crown returns to claim Bess, he and Porgy fight, and Crown is killed. Sportin' Life convinces Bess that Porgy will be put in jail forever and that she ought to go off to New York with him. She agrees. But Porgy returns and is determined not to lose her. Optimistically, he sets off to find her, riding in his little wagon drawn by a goat.

As Sportin' Life, Sammy Davis is a flashy, evil little man who sells "happy dust" and liquor to the folks on Catfish Row. Pearl Bailey plays Maria and Diahann Carroll is Clara, two of the women who befriend Bess.

As in *Carmen Jones*, the singing voices of the principle performers were dubbed. Bess is sung by Adele Addison, Porgy by Robert McFerrin, and Clara by Loulie Jean Norman.

Sportin' Life

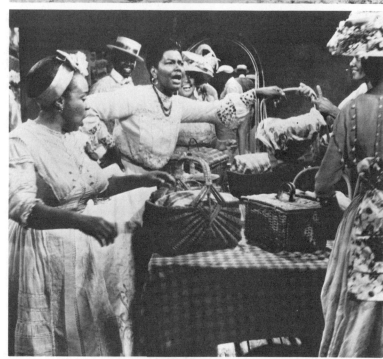

Left: Pearl Bailey as Maria and other Catfish Row women prepare for a Sunday picnic. Above: Crown (left) and Porgy (right) fight over Bess. Crown is killed.

Eartha Kitt

Eartha Kitt and Sammy Davis in Anna Lucasta (1958)

"I'm special," Eartha Kitt told an interviewer. "A special type. When you're too special or too good, people don't know what to do with you. They categorize you. They put you into a slot."

Catlike, exotic, silky, smoldering, expensive—that's Eartha Kitt's slot. Her trademark is slinky sex appeal, and her name seems too perfect to be anything but a press agent's invention.

But that's what her mother named her, she says, when she was born in a town called North in South Carolina in 1928. Her early years were not happy ones. "I'll never forget how my own people treated me and my Mother. I had reddish hair and I was too light. Everybody called me 'that yellow girl' and nobody wanted me, Negro or white." When she was eight she went to live in Harlem with an aunt. "When I arrived in Pennsylvania Station," she wrote, "I wore an identification tag and carried two catfish sandwiches. I was afraid the tall buildings would fall on me. There were two hundred of us back in my cotton patch. . . . New York was incredible. . . . I saw my first electric light, my first bathroom and my first telephone. I guess I was a pretty ignorant kid. I thought little men played music inside the gramophone."

She learned quickly. After attending the High School of Performing Arts, she joined the Katherine Dunham dancers, with whom she studied, learned African and Haitian songs, and toured throughout Europe. When the troupe returned to the United States, she remained in Paris, booked into a fashionable night club called Carroll's. She returned during the early fifties and appeared at La Vie en Rose, the Village Vanguard, and the Blue Angel.

Eartha Kitt sings in St. Louis Blues (1958). Nat King Cole is at the piano.

Real fame came to her when she appeared on Broadway in Leonard Stillman's *New Faces of 1952*. Draped across a silk chaise lounge, wearing elegant velvet knee-breaches, she sang in a weary, silky voice, "Though Chiang Kai-shek sends me pots of tea; T. S. Elliot writes books for me; Sherman Billingsley cooks for me . . . I could not be wearier . . . Life could not be drearier . . ." The song was called "Monotonous" and Eartha Kitt was a sensation. She appeared in the movie version. Then came offers from night clubs, three more Broadway shows, records and film contracts, and along with them a wardrobe designed in Paris, which reportedly cost $25,000, diamonds and mink, dinner engagements with

Nehru and Albert Einstein, romances with Orson Welles, Salvador Dali, Porfirio Rubirosa. Her night club theme song was something titled "I Want to Be Evil." One of her record albums is titled *The Bad Eartha.*

Her feline typecasting was incredible. She starred in the road company of *The Owl and the Pussycat* with Russell Nype; played Batman's Catwoman on television; and in 1957, starred as a sinful, lovable alley cat named Mehitabel in *Shinbone Alley,* a Broadway musical adaptation of Don Marquis's *Archy and Mehitabel.*

In 1968 she made the headlines in an entirely different way. Because of work she had been doing in Watts, she was invited to a White House luncheon given by Lady Bird Johnson. The topic for discussion was "What citizens can do to insure safe streets," and the proceedings were very ladylike—until she stood up. "I have to say what is in my heart," she began, addressing her criticism to Mrs. Johnson and, by implication, to the entire Johnson administration. "You send the best of this country off to be shot and maimed. . . . They rebel in the streets."

Mrs. Johnson replied, "I am sorry I cannot understand the things that you do. I have not lived with the background that you have."

Her outburst won Eartha Kitt an editorial in the *New York Times*. It said in part, "Even those, black, brown, or yellow who have managed to achieve every outward success in the white man's world bear the psychic scars of centuries of injustice. When the old wounds are reopened . . . all the accumulated venom of the ages pours out. . . . It is there and it must be faced."

At a recent appearance at the fashionable Persian Room of the Plaza hotel, the elegant Eartha Kitt stood in the spotlight and sang softly:

> "Brown baby, brown baby
> As you grow up
> I want you to drink
> From the plenty cup . . ."

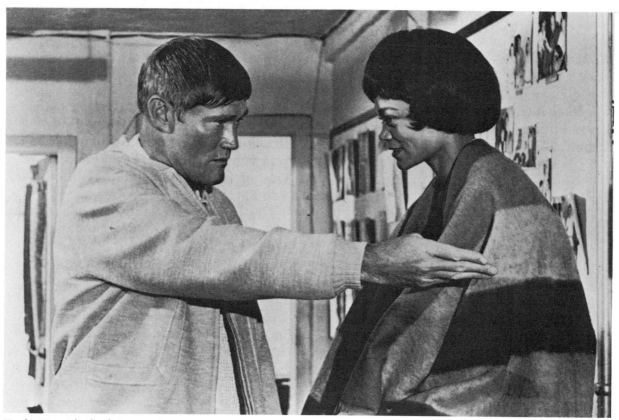

Eartha Kitt with Chuck Connors in Synanon (1965)

Ossie Davis

Left: Ossie Davis (center) as Father Gillis in The Cardinal (1963)
Right: Ossie Davis as Purlie Victorious and Ruby Dee as
Lutiebelle in Gone Are the Days! (1964)

"I'm tired of being a show-business civil rights leader," Ossie Davis once told an interviewer. "The spokesman side of you soon swallows up the artist."

But after Martin Luther King was assassinated Davis was forced to "make a long examination" of himself: "Was I doing enough to further the image of black manhood in this country?" Davis no longer worries about his dual role as an artist and civil rights spokesman. "Both roads are closer together than I realized."

Ossie Davis was born in Cogdell, Georgia. His father was a railroad engineer, an unusual job for a black in the deep South. His mother "carried a pistol in her bosom to protect her five children." After finishing high school in Waycross, Georgia, Davis hitchhiked north and enrolled in Howard University, hoping to become a playwright. After two years he left college and went to New York, where he hoped to earn his living by writing. He found this was not possible, and he worked first as a janitor, next as a stock clerk, and then pushed a handcart in the garment district.

He joined a Harlem theatre group, but shortly thereafter was drafted, serving in the medical corps in West Africa and later transferred to the special services, where he wrote and produced several shows, one titled Goldbrickers of 1944. After his discharge he was living in Valdosta, Georgia, when he received an offer to appear on Broadway in Robert Ardrey's play Jeb opposite Ruby Dee. He toured with her in Anna Lucasta and in 1949, during the run of The Smile of the World, they were married.

His first film was No Way Out (1950). During the fifties he continued to appear in small roles in films and on Broadway. He appeared in Jamaica with Lena Horne and later replaced Sidney Poitier in the Broadway production of A Raisin in the Sun. His one-act play Alice in Wonder, dealing with the politics of the McCarthy era, was produced in Harlem in 1953.

In 1961 playwright Davis brought his own work, Purlie Victorious, to Broadway. Starring in it along with Ruby Dee and Godfrey Cambridge, he played all the stereotypes—this time for comedy. Two years later they did it all over again in the film version, titled *Gone Are the Days.*

Davis did a movie a year during the sixties. In 1970 he was hired to play Coffin Ed Johnson in *Cotton Comes to Harlem.* The producer asked him to look over the script and make some changes, when, he explained, "I was finally sidetracked and sandbagged into rewriting the whole script." He was later named director and Raymond St. Jacques was hired to replace him as Coffin Ed. The next year Davis and others founded a group called Third World Cinema Corporation, aimed at increasing the opportunities for blacks and Puerto Ricans in movies. The same year, he directed *Kongi's Harvest,* made in Nigeria, in cooperation with that country's fledgling movie industry, and in 1972 he directed *Black Girl,* one of the most genuine of the new "black interest" films.

Davis in The Slaves (1969)

He was chairman of the Angela Davis Defense Fund and delivered eulogies at the funerals of both Malcolm X and Martin Luther King. About Malcolm he said, "[He] was our manhood, our living, black manhood! . . . And in honoring him, we honor the best in ourselves."

Asked why his career has not resulted in a "Poitier-like" stardom, Davis told interviewer Nat Hentoff: "There are ways you can make yourself a more saleable commodity. I didn't pursue those ways. My wife and I did build careers for ourselves and in the process did many theatrical things . . . on street corners, churches, union halls, schools. And in doing it our way, we didn't have to sell more of ourselves than we could get back before the sun went down . . . ."

Ruby
Dee

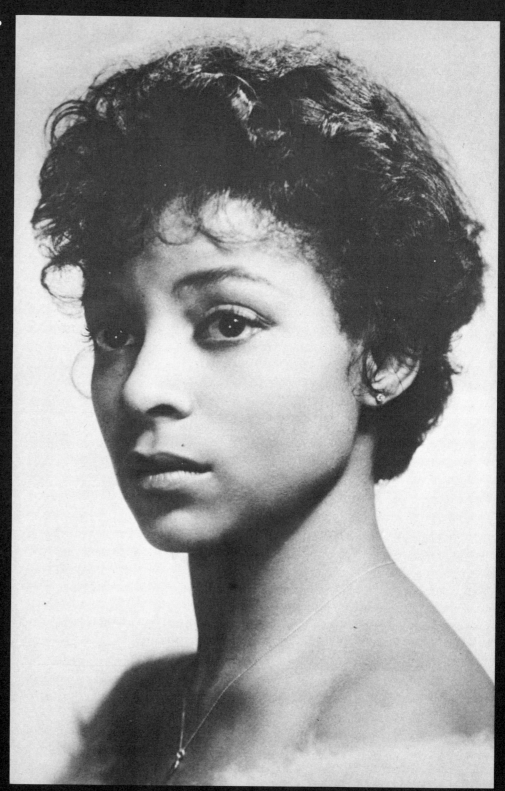

Ruby Dee and Jackie Robinson in The Jackie Robinson Story *(1950)*

Ruby Dee and Johnny Nash in Take a Giant Step *(1960)*

"After each new thing I do," Ruby Dee has said, "people tell me I'm really on my way. Maybe one day, I'll actually arrive."

Ruby Dee is a dramatic actress and comedienne. She is tiny, delicate, and beautiful. She has never had a bad review. If she has not exactly "arrived" in the Hollywood sense, it may be because, as she puts it, "There have been few, if any great parts written for black actresses. Up until now, the best have been roles like Ethel Waters' in *The Member of the Wedding* or the mother in *A Raisin in the Sun*. But that isn't the black woman today."

Today's black woman is the part Ruby Dee wants to portray. And her progress from the smiling, loyal, uncomplaining girls of her early films to Tank Williams' woman in *Up Tight!* and Sidney Poitier's in *Buck and the Preacher* has been interesting to observe. Born in Cleveland, Ruby Dee Wallace was a year old when her family moved to Harlem, where she learned "what a ghetto was." Her father was a porter and waiter for the Pennsylvania Railroad; her mother a school teacher. She attended Hunter High School, a laboratory school for "bright" children, and later Hunter College. But it was her work and study with the American Negro Theatre that laid the foundation for her life and her career. *Anna Lucasta,* originally an American Negro

Theatre production, took her to Broadway in 1946. She later married her fellow student and co-star Ossie Davis.

In *The Jackie Robinson Story* (1950), *Go Man Go* (1954), *Edge of the City* (1957), *St. Louis Blues* (1958), and *Take a Giant Step* (1961), she played the essence of sweetness and virtue. As Sidney Poitier's long-suffering pregnant wife in *A Raisin in the Sun* (1961), the critics agreed she was what her mother had always hoped she'd be—"something special." She said in an interview, "Starting with the American Negro Theatre productions, I have played Sidney's wife a dozen times, although my memory is inexact. I have played my own husband's wife four or five times."

Her role in *The Balcony* (1963) took her "out of gingham"—she played a prostitute. She went on to establish herself as a comedienne as Lutiebelle in her husband's play *Purlie Victorious* and in the 1963 movie version called *Gone Are the Days*. She widened her range even further as both co-author and co-star of the film *Up Tight!* (1968), the first full-length film treatment of black militancy. *Up Tight!* is the story of Tank Williams, a jobless alcoholic and militant-turned-informer. "Tank is dead when you meet

him," she says. "He is defeated by the society and the times in which we live. He is defeated by his own inability to make choices which stems from a kind of hysteric de-gutting."

She and Davis have shared strong humanitarian and political interests in dozens of causes, including SNCC, the Young Lords, the Black Panthers, the NAACP, and community drug prevention programs. Friends of both Malcolm X and Martin Luther King, Ruby Dee and her husband were recipients of the Urban League's Frederick Douglass Award in 1970.

Ruby Dee has appeared in many stage productions, most recently with James Earl Jones in the off-Broadway play, *Boesmann and Lena*. As Lena, a South African woman and "a total victim of a system," she received what the *New York Times* called "the most dazzling personal notices of the season." In 1972 she played Poitier's courageous and eloquent woman in *Buck and the Preacher*. Though *Variety* praised the film generally and Ruby Dee's performance in particular, the review added, "Someday, Miss Dee will get a part worthy of her." Which is another way of saying "she's really on her way."

James Earl Jones

James Earl Jones was born in Mississippi and was adopted and raised by his maternal grandparents on a farm near Mainstee, Michigan. As a child he developed a stammer so crippling he was often able to communicate only by writing. Determination, practice, and a place on the debating team overcame this, so that by the time he graduated from high school the stammer had disappeared.

At the University of Michigan on a scholarship, he planned to study medicine but switched to drama. After graduation he joined the army, where his specialty was mountain warfare, and he briefly considered becoming a regular army officer. Instead, he moved to New York to live with his father, prizefighter-turned-actor Robert Earl Jones. Taking advantage of the G.I. Bill, he studied at the American Theatre Wing for two years. At night, he and his father waxed floors.

He has appeared in eighteen off-Broadway productions including one in which his father also appeared, *Moon on a Rainbow Shawl*. On Broadway he played in *Sunrise at Campobello* and *The Cool World*.

Beginning in 1960, he appeared for seven consecutive summers with Joseph Papp's New York Shakespeare Festival, where his most important role was Othello in 1964. After the Central Park production the show moved to the Martinique Theater, off-Broadway. He followed Othello with a stint as an "oversized and impotent" African chieftain in the *Tarzan* series on television, worked in television soap operas, toured Europe in *The Emperor Jones*, and then played his first movie role as the bombardier in *Dr. Strangelove* (1963).

When *The Great White Hope* pre-

James Earl Jones with Elizabeth Taylor and Richard Burton in The Comedians (1967)

miered on Broadway, Jones, who had shaved his head and trained for the part like a prizefighter, won an ovation from the audience and rave notices from the critics. He went on to recreate the role in the 1970 film and win an Oscar nomination.

In *The Man* (1970), originally shot by ABC as a made-for-television movie, he played the first black president of the United States. That same year he appeared with Ruby Dee in the Circle-in-the-Square production of *Boesmann and*

Lena as Boesmann, a South African native and "totally mutilated person."

Jones is currently host and producer of *Black Omnibus*, a weekly, hour-long television show devoted entirely to the arts.

In public, James Earl Jones prefers to show a low profile. "I'm not recognized on the street and that's the way I want it," he told an interviewer. "I prefer to be recognized for fine work. There is only one thing I demand. And that is total attention when I'm on stage while I am performing and total privacy when I'm not."

Left: Jones as Doctor D in End of the Road (1969)
Above: Jones as the president of the United States in The Man (1972)

Godfrey Cambridge

Marty Ingels and Godfrey Cambridge in The Busy Body *(1967)*

Godfrey Cambridge claims to have worked as a popcorn bunny maker, a hot-rod racer, a gardener, a bouncer in a saloon, an airplane wing cleaner, a maternity hospital ambulance driver, a judo instructor (he's a brown belt), a bead sorter, a freelance drama critic, and as a paid "laugher" for Broadway and television shows. He has also put in a lot of time behind the wheel of a taxicab. ("I told Lena Horne she can't get a cab because she looks too shifty.")

Out of the depths of this experience, he views himself as "champion of the little guy." He has taken on New York City's Hack Bureau ("I've caused a few headlines by doing unorthodox things. Like trying to go home ") and hallowed institutions such as commercial laundries and the telephone company ("I spindle and staple whenever I can").

Godfrey Cambridge's parents came to Harlem from British Guiana during the Depression. His father dug up streets for Con Edison and his mother was a garment worker. He was born in 1933. Most of his early years were spent in Nova Scotia with his grandparents. ("My mother sent me there to miss the Harlem schools.") At thirteen he came home and went to high school in Flushing, New York, where his class yearbook called him "Unforgetable Godfrey Wonder Boy Cambridge." He won a scholarship to Hofstra and established himself as a campus big wheel. Encountering racial prejudice, he dropped out. "I'm a guy who worked hard, studied hard, and was a nice guy in college. . . . Then I found out what it means to be black in America—and did twenty years of growing in six months. Now I talk about it!"

Godfrey Cambridge and Davy Kay enjoy a pizza picnic in The Biggest Bundle of Them All *(1968).*

He was offered the part of the bartender in *Take a Giant Step* off-Broadway: "They wanted to give me ten dollars a week. I asked for fifteen because my 'artistic endeavors' included playing the part, sweeping the floor, and moving the piano. I wasn't going to get a hernia for ten dollars a week." In 1956 he entered a laughing contest and was voted one of the four laugh champions of the United States. The title led to an appearance on *I've Got a Secret* and the "laugher" job.

His first Broadway part in *Mr. Johnson* was written out of the show shortly before it opened. In the 1959 movie, *The Last Angry Man*, he played a young hood-

lum named Nobody Home. Then in 1961 he appeared in the off-Broadway production of *The Blacks*, played a white woman who was raped and murdered, and won an Obie for the effort. The same year, he was featured in *Purlie Victorious* on Broadway and Jack Paar invited him to appear on his show. ("I owe it all to Jack Paar. I was a Negro and I had a new approach to comedy. All the networks were afraid of me because anything new always arouses a great deal of timidity. But Paar had the courage to say, 'We go.' The first show was taped on Lincoln's birthday. That's symbolic . . . I got my freedom to perform.") His Paar appearance

Estelle Parsons (left) and Godfrey Cambridge (right) as the white man who . . .
wakes up one morning to discover he has turned black, in The Watermelon Man *(1970).*

led to a recording contract, movie roles, and other television bookings. ("TV can be a strain. Everybody in it is trying to protect his house in Greenwich.")

Between 1967 and 1969 he lost 170 pounds ("I've got letters on my ice box turning me down for parts. Face it, there are no Sidney Greenstreet roles any more"), and then appeared in Melvin Van Peebles' *Watermelon Man* (1970) as Jeff Gerber, a white bigot who wakes up one morning to discover he has turned black, and as the detective, Grave Digger Jones, in *Cotton Comes to Harlem* (1970), a role he repeated in the sequel, *Come Back Charleston Blue* (1972).

Cambridge dislikes what he calls "sacrificial lamb" movies, in which the black always dies ("I don't want to be Jesus; its very painful for my palms"); says he is not nonviolent ("When you hit me over the head, I have a lot of trouble keeping in tune with the freedom song"); and rejects the label of racial satirist ("That's not my bag. Let's just say I deal in universal human foibles").

On a cold day in January 1961 John F. Kennedy stood in front of the Capitol Building and said, "Let the word go forth from this time and place that the torch has been passed to a new generation of Americans. . . . So let us begin anew." With these words, Kennedy marked the end of what had been an age of apathy and ushered in a new decade of caring, striving, commitment. But it was also a decade of tearing violence and drama. Before three years were over, the man who had announced the new day and stood as its living symbol would also become its victim.

On February 1, 1960, four students from North Carolina Agricultural and Technical College sat down at the local Woolworth store in Greensboro to have a cup of coffee. As they had expected, it was denied them because of their color. They remained seated, insistent on their rights; ultimately they won them. The sit-ins had begun in earnest. As a technique of protest they would spread through the country like wildfire. By 1963 it is estimated that 70,000 blacks and whites had sat in or protested at over 800 establishments in over 200 cities with more than 6,000 arrests, desegregating restaurants in at least 100 locales.

But halfway around the world, an elite corps of a few hundred Americans were engaged in training the army of South Vietnam to fight an American war against so-called Communist aggression. The effects of this action, too, would spread like wildfire throughout the nation and the world.

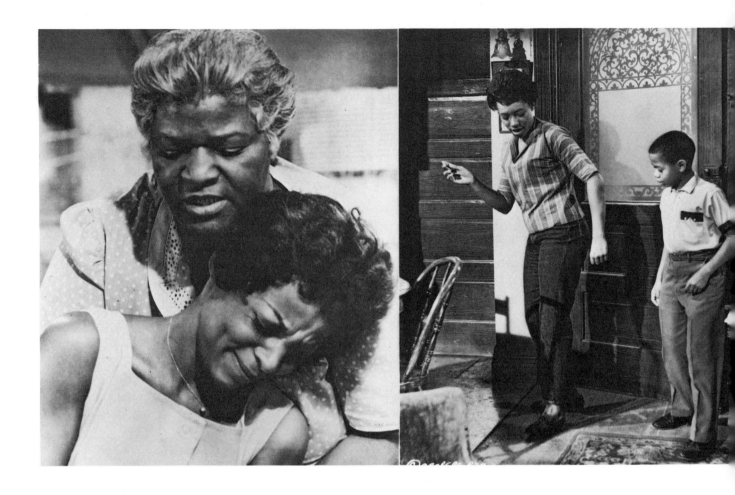

A Raisin in the Sun

Shortly after the close of Lorraine Hansberry's long-running play, *A Raisin in the Sun*, the cast went to Hollywood to put the play on film. The result stands as a testimony to the end of the ideal of integration.

Raisin is the story of the matriarch Lena Younger (Claudia McNeil) and the life of her family in their tiny ghetto apartment. Sidney Poitier is her bitter, restless son, Walter, who sees nothing ahead of him except a lifetime of being a chauffeur; Ruby Dee is his pregnant,

long-suffering wife, Ruth; Diana Sands is her youngest daughter, Beneatha, a wise-cracking, intellectual medical student; Stephen Perry is her grandson, child of Walter and Ruth. Lena's husband has died and left the family his great gift—life insurance benefits of $10,000. Lena hopes to use this money to help her family escape the ghetto, and she uses part of it to put a down payment on a house in the white suburbs where, she believes, things will be better for them.

Walter wants to invest the rest of the

Left to right: Claudia McNeil comforts her daughter-in-law, Ruby Dee; Diana Sands, as Beneatha Younger, teaches her nephew Travis (Stephen Perry) how to dance; The Youngers pack to move from their ghetto apartment to a home in the suburbs.

money in a liquor store. Lena refuses, saying her husband's memory will not be invested in liquor. Walter begs, pleads, and storms. Finally, seeing that he is being destroyed, Lena gives him the money, telling him to use all but that needed to pay Beneatha's medical school tuition, and the family prepares to move "to the sun." Walter then discovers that his liquor store partner has run away with the family's money, including Beneatha's tuition. Meanwhile, a hostile "welcoming committee" from the new neighbor-hood has come to call, offering to buy the Younger's new house from them at a profit if only they do not move in. Walter, who has grown stronger as a result of the financial disaster, refuses. When the film ends, the family is preparing to take on the burdens of their new white neighborhood.

Lorraine Hansberry died a few years after the film was made. Had she lived, it would have been fascinating to see her write the story of the Younger family ten years later.

Diana Sands

In *A Raisin in the Sun* Diana Sands was named Broadway's Best Supporting Actress; in *Blues for Mister Charlie* she "lit up 52nd Street" and "sent shivers through hundreds of spines"; in *Tiger Tiger Burning Bright* she was a "bewitching virtuoso"; in *The Owl and the Pussycat* "a most provocative and dynamic young actress." In short, Diana Sands has had the kinds of theatre reviews actresses dream of. But after each Broadway triumph, instead of finding herself in the permanent ranks of stardom, she has found herself out of work.

"When I first started out in the theatre," she says "I had all the illusions. But after a year of making the rounds, I found I just couldn't make rounds any more. I'd sleep until four in the afternoon to avoid it and then I figured I'd better give up the illusions. Finally, on the New York opening night of *Raisin* I thought it would be all right to have those illusions again." But two years after completing the play and winning raves, going on to make her first big film appearance in *Raisin* and following it with an important role in *An Affair of the Skin* (1963), Diana Sands found herself back in Hollywood playing a native girl in a South Seas comedy, *Ensign Pulver,* a tiny part with no billing.

Diana Sands was born in the Bronx in 1934 and lived in Harlem and Westchester. Her father was a carpenter; her mother a milliner. "When I was about six, my brother took me to a Dorothy Lamour movie, *The Road to Hope* or something. When we got home, I wrapped a towel around me and said, 'Thomas, do I look like her?' Then after that, I always would entertain when we had people in . . . . I also painted and wrote and when it came time to go to high school, I couldn't decide whether to go to Performing Arts or Music and Art. For Mu-

Diana Sands as a native girl in Ensign Pulver *(1964)*

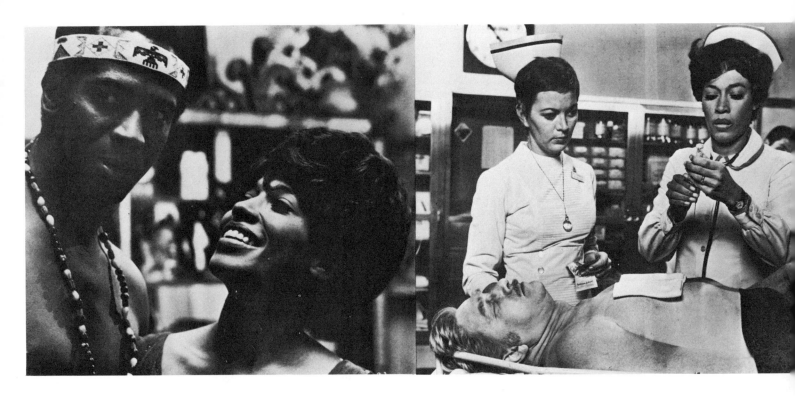

sic and Art you had to do twenty paintings, but for Performing Arts you only had to do two monologues. I guess I was lazy."

After graduating from Performing Arts High School where she was named Best Actress in her senior year, she joined the Charles A. Taylor Show, a carnival, about which she reports, "I sang 'Sentimental Journey' and thought I was *the cheese.*" A year later, she was half of the team of "Twan and Diana," an oriental dance team "complete with bells and veils." When there was no work at all, she did a market research survey and filled out survey cards to be sent on to IBM key punch operators.

Meanwhile, she was making theatrical rounds and, from time to time, getting work. After half a dozen minor roles she became discouraged about a career in the theatre. Remembering those IBM key punch cards, she borrowed a few hundred dollars and went to key punch school. Just as she was completing the probation period on her job, she was offered a part in *Land Beyond the River* off-Broadway for fifteen dollars a week.

Left to right: Lou Gossett and Diana Sands in The Landlord *(1970); Diana Sands in* Doctor's Wives *(1971); Diana Sands with Dirk Benedict in* Georgia, Georgia *(1972)*

She grabbed it.

Her first Broadway performance was that of Beneatha Younger in *A Raisin in the Sun*, which she then recreated in the 1961 film. She then spent six months out of work. She alternated between off-Broadway, Broadway, Hollywood, and television, receiving Obie awards and Tony nominations one year and offers of walk-ons as a maid the next.

Sands toured extensively during the middle sixties, playing Lady Macbeth, Cleopatra, Phaedra, and Medea with repertory theatres all over the country and appearing in *Born Yesterday, Wait Until Dark,* and *Two for the Seesaw.* In 1967, she came to the Repertory Theater at Lincoln Center in New York as *Saint Joan* and as Cassandra in *Tiger at the Gates. The Landlord* (1970) was her first important film role in ten years. Then came the movie soap opera, *Doctor's Wives* (1971), and finally the odd-but-fascinating *Georgia, Georgia* in 1972.

Diana Sands once told an interviewer, "The worst thing that can happen to a person is to give up—or settle in." So far, she seems to have done neither.

The 1960s were a time in which the young conscience of a nation tried to come to terms with technology, ecology, and human rights. Technology would give us the capability to control the "mind" of a computer, the energy of the laser, and the explosive power of rockets which stood taller than a thirty-story building; it would enable us to live under the sea, to look down at our world from outer space, and ultimately to plant the flag of our country on the surface of the moon. But increasingly difficult problems of land, air, and water pollution set us to wondering what we, our corporations, and our government were doing to the natural world around us. New organizations—such as the Black Panthers, Women's Liberation, and Students for a Democratic Society (SDS)—prodded us to think about the place our society offered senior citizens, women, the young, the poor, and the minorities.

In May 1961 James Farmer, the director of CORE, led a group of blacks and whites in a long series of bus rides known as Freedom Rides, throughout the South.

The Civil Rights Act of 1964 (and the Voting Rights Act of 1965 which corrected some of its defects) was the legislative result of the civil rights decade. It ruled against segregation and discrimination in voting, education, and public accommodations, with broad federal powers of enforcement. Many whites began to feel the country had "gone too far" and blacks had been "given too much" and the "white backlash" began. As a result, black struggles took new forms and directions.

The event which sparked the passage of the 1964 Civil Rights Act was the August 1963 march on Washington, where 250,000 people met to protest discrimination and mark the hundred-year anniversary of the Emancipation Proclamation. They listened to Dr. Martin Luther King speak of his dream, a simple dream of personal dignity for all men. Malcolm X called it the "farce on Washington" and stated that once again blacks had been hoaxed by whites: "inevitably, the black man's anger rekindled, deeper than ever, and there began bursting out in different cities, in the 'long, hot summer' of 1964, unprecedented racial crises."

At the same time, millions of people stood to speak out against the war in Vietnam and against those unable to respect one another's dreams. But the war went on. By the middle of

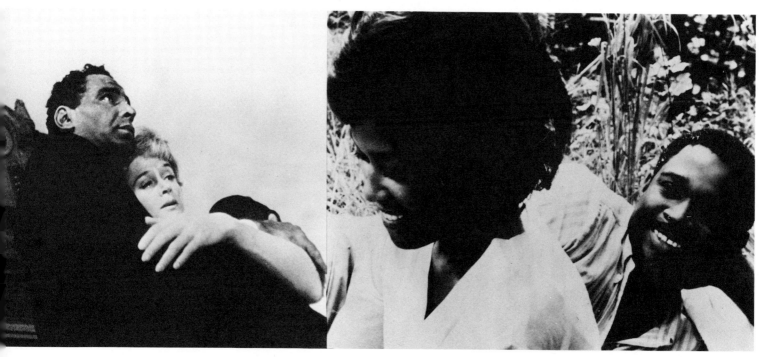

the sixties, blacks had begun to realize that despite new laws and programs, racial discrimination was going on, too. They responded with the Black Power movement, in its various forms. The Nation of Islam, or the Black Muslims, advocated and practiced black capitalism, black-owned and operated businesses. So did CORE. Some groups, including SNCC, concentrated on forming and winning recognition of black political parties in Alabama and Mississippi, while others emphasized cultural nationalism in art and education. The Black Panthers armed themselves to fight back and went into the community with breakfast and medical programs.

In 1968, President Johnson signed the Fair Housing Act, outlawing racial discrimination in the sale and rental of apartments and houses. That year, with the election of President Nixon, marked the end of the civil rights decade.

Early in 1971, the Black Caucus of the House of Representatives again tried to "work within the system," presenting demands for reform in welfare, job discrimination, job placement, social justice, and school segregation. They considered Nixon's responses "minimal"; answering one of the most urgent demands, a guaranteed annual income of $6,500, the president recommended $2,400.

Jim Brown

If there really is a "door" and if Sidney Poitier really opened it, then Jim Brown may have been the first to stride all the way through. He comes on as a tough, courageous, bare-chested Saturday afternoon matinee hero and says, "I don't want to play Negro parts. Just cool, tough modern men who are also Negroes. And not good guys all the time."

In real life Brown is a cool-headed money man whose investments are well diversified and include a publishing company, a record company, a movie company, a music management company, a night club, a ski lodge, a cosmetics firm, substantial real estate, and a prizefight investment group.

He was born James Nathaniel Brown on St. Simon's Island off the coast of Georgia in 1935, and moved to Long Island's Spinney Hill, the black ghetto which lies between the affluent communities of Great Neck and Manhasset, when he was seven. His mother was a housekeeper for a Great Neck family and his father, Swinton "Sweet Sue" Brown, "would be there for a while and then not there."

As the star athlete and pride of Manhasset High School, he had a roster of local "boosters," men important in the local community whose encouragement helped him to win a scholarship to Syracuse University. There he made All-American in both football and lacrosse. He played nine seasons as star fullback of the Cleveland Browns and gained more yardage than anyone in the history of pro football. After a pro bowl game in the early sixties, Brown was approached by a Hollywood producer who suggested he take a screen test. He was cast in *Rio Conchos* (1964) and did so well in rehearsal that his part was built up to that of co-star. During the filming of his next movie, *The Dirty Dozen* (1967), he an-

Jim Brown in Rio Conchos (1964)

159

nounced that he was quitting football.

In both *The Dirty Dozen* and *Dark of the Sun* (1968), Brown dies gracefully: "My parts are somewhat limited . . . . I'd like to make a film in which I get the girl and live happily ever after." *100 Rifles* (1968) was his eighth movie in three years; "This is a new day. I get the chick," he announced happily. He lives, but "the chick," Raquel Welch, dies.

Marvin Schwartz, the producer of *100 Rifles*, called him "a natural" and said, "He goes on instinct. He dominates the screen and he has tremendous sex appeal." In each succeeding film he seems to become more and more the hero. *The Split* (1968) has been called the first real black superhero film. Though all the white men who conspire with him to steal the receipts of a pro football game die, Brown, the superior man, lives to fight again. By the time he appears in *Black Gunn* (1972), he has become the total black superhero, who is wronged, wants revenge, and gets it.

Brown believes that black power equals green power and is a founder and president of the Black Economic Union, a nonprofit corporation organized to help black business with low-interest loans, marketing advice, and contact with the white establishment. He describes himself as "free and black": "I'm supposed to be arrogant and supposed to be militant. I swing loose and free and have been outspoken on racial matters. And I don't preach against black militant groups. I'm not humble."

Opposite: Brown in The Dirty Dozen (1967)

Left: Brown with Raquel Welch in 100 Rifles (1968)
Below: Brown with Yvette Mimieux in Dark of the Sun (1968)

Raymond St. Jacques and Alec Guinness in The Comedians *(1967)*

Raymond St. Jacques

Raymond St. Jacques was born James Arthur Johnson in 1930 in Hartford, Connecticut. His parents were divorced, and his mother worked as a domestic. While he was in high school, she took college courses, became a medical technician, and paid his way to Yale, where he majored in psychology, planning to be a social worker. But a friend suggested he audition for the leading role in a local production of Othello, and he was into the theatre for good. After college it was Shakespeare and more Shakespeare—in New York, San Diego, and at Stratford, Connecticut, where he also taught fencing and staged the duels. He tried all sorts of stage names, searching for one that would "fill up a page." He finally settled for Raymond St. Jacques, the name of a boy he had once known in Hartford.

After moving to New York, he worked as a salesman in Bloomingdale's, a male model, a dishwasher, a stockboy, a houseboy in Scarsdale, and a costume jewelry salesman. Finally, in 1954 he got a part in an off-Broadway production, *High Name Today.* When the director first turned him down, saying there were no parts in the play for blacks, St. Jacques reminded him that the play was about American soldiers in Korea and that blacks had been there too. He was hired. He studied at Actor's Studio and began to get steady work in the theatre and bit parts on television. In 1961 he appeared in *The Blacks* with Godfrey Cambridge, Cicely Tyson, and James Earl Jones. His first film was *Black Like Me* in 1964.

St. Jacques holds one of those "first black actor to—" titles. His appearance as Simon Blake in *Rawhide* made him the first black actor to appear regularly in a featured role in a television series. The newspaper headlines read, "St. Jacques of B'way Breaks Color Line Among TV Cowboys." Later he said, "All I amounted to on that show was tokenism."

He began to receive movie offers and appeared in *Mr. Moses* (1965), *Mr. Buddwing* (1965), *Madigan* (1968), and *The Green Berets* (1968). Speaking of his role in *The Green Berets*, he told an interviewer, "I tried to find justification. I hoped to integrate the film. I took the role for money; I was a little confused. When I saw a preview, I wanted to join the pickets downstairs." But things got better: He was nominated for an Acad-

emy Award for his part in *The Comedians* (1967) and received star billing in *Up Tight!* (1968) as B.G., the teacher-turned-militant who believes guns are the only solution.

After appearing in *Cotton Comes to Harlem* (1970), *Cool Breeze* (1970), and *Come Back Charleston Blue* (1972), St. Jacques decided to produce and direct his own picture. He chose Robert Pharr's novel *Book of Numbers* for the script. He calls *Book of Numbers* (1973) the "first black nostalgia film" and says, "If I fall on my ass, it's still a step forward. I won't fall that way again. People put down Stepin Fetchit. He paid his dues. Because of him there could be Poitier. Because of Poitier, I'm here. It's a question of what you have to do to survive and you had to bend a lot more in 1930 than you do now. That's what the movie is about, in a way."

Above left: St. Jacques with Juanita Moore in Uptight! *(1969)*
Above right: St. Jacques as Coffin Ed Johnson in Cotton Comes to Harlem *(1970)   Above: More of the same in* Come Back Charleston Blue *(1972)*

Calvin Lockhart

"I'm very much in sympathy with the Panthers," Calvin Lockhart once said, "and very much against a civilization that causes the necessity of a Black Panther organization."

Calvin Lockhart is a militant, but not a pasteboard, one-dimensional militant. He is able to understand complexity and able to portray it. He is an actor who is also a black. He is a black who is also an actor. During the filming of a school riot in *Halls of Anger* (1970), Lockhart's part called for him to jump on a truck and yell, "Black ain't right and white ain't right; only right is right." Lockhart refused, commenting in a later interview, "It's a beautiful line, but it's so damned wrong."

He was born in Nassau in 1934, the oldest of eight children. His father was a musician, able to play eight different instruments; his mother sold straw baskets to tourists. He learned carpentry in Nassau and by helping to build houses saved enough money to come to New York and enroll in Cooper Union as an engineering student. After a year he switched to acting and supported himself between parts by driving a cab and working as a carpenter.

Lockhart's first part was in *Dark of the Moon* at the Harlem YMCA, with Cicely Tyson. He came to Broadway in *The Cool World* and *A Taste of Honey*. His next eight years were spent in Europe and his work on BBC television led to a starring role as the black nightclub owner in the British film *Joanna*, which was released here in 1968. Back in this country in 1970, he won parts in four films, *Halls of Anger, Myra Breckenridge, Leo the Last,* and *Cotton Comes to Harlem*. The range and dimension of his portrayals—from the ghetto hero in *Leo* to the sequined-haired queen in *Myra*—seem to guarantee him an important future in Hollywood. In 1972 he played the disc jockey, Frankie J. Parker, in *Melinda*, which exemplifies a new kind of film—the black man triumphant. *Variety* prophesied "strong box office while the trend lasts."

Lockhart has helped to found a creative arts center in Nassau which offers workshops in writing, dance, music and art. As to his view of the future, he said in a recent interview that he would like to become a producer of "films that will uproot cherished beliefs and make the powers-that-be very unhappy."

Left: Calvin Lockhart in Leo the Last (1970)
as a teacher in Halls of Anger (1970)   *Below: Lockhart*

Left: Lockhart plays the Reverend Deke O'Malley in Cotton
Comes to Harlem (1970), with Emily Yancy.   Above: Lockhart
with Raquel Welch in Myra Breckenridge (1970)

Opposite top: Shirley Knight taunts Al Freeman Jr. in Dutchman (1967), the Le Roi Jones drama describing a black man's destruction   Opposite bottom: Juano Hernandez (left) in his last film appearance, with Rod Steiger (right) in The Pawnbroker (1965)   Above: Blacks take over an advertising agency in Putney Swope (1969), a spoof of white business practices.

Gordon Parks

"The full meaning of Momma's death had settled over me before they lowered her into the grave," Gordon Parks wrote in his autobiography, *A Choice of Weapons*. "They buried her at two-thirty in the afternoon and at nightfall our big family was starting to break up. Once there had been fifteen of us and, at sixteen, I was the youngest. There was never much money, so my older brothers and sisters were scraping up enough for my coach ticket north. I would live in St. Paul, Minnesota, with my sister Maggie Lee, as my mother had requested a few minutes before she died."

Born in 1920, Gordon Parks was sixteen when he left Fort Scott, Kansas, to live with his sister. He did not stay long; after a disagreement with his brother-in-law, he moved out and was on his own, earning his first money by working as a piano player in a whorehouse. Struggling to support himself and finish high school, he washed dishes and worked at odd jobs, including cleaning bathrooms in a flophouse. When he had nothing for room rent, he slept on trolleys. He finally gave up the idea of finishing school and concentrated on staying alive. During a stint as a busboy in a St. Paul hotel, he sneaked into the ballroom after hours to play the piano. The band leader, Larry Duncan, heard him and hired him. After a tour, the band broke up in New York and as Parks later described it he was "sort of vomited out into Harlem."

After more odd jobs, Parks joined the Civilian Conservation Corps and worked at clearing forest land. At twenty-four he had become a railroad dining car waiter, and during a layover in Chicago he bought a camera for $12.50. His pictures were displayed at a photo shop and he was offered work as a fashion pho-

Kyle Johnson and Carole Lemond in The Learning Tree (1969)

tographer for a department store. He moved to Chicago and continued to learn about the camera and darkroom technique. Joe Louis' wife hired him to photograph her, other portrait work followed, and Parks' income had soon jumped to $150 a day, but he was not satisfied with that sort of work; he applied for and won a Julius Rosenwald Fellowship in photography. During World War II he worked at the Office of War Information and later as a industrial cameraman for Standard Oil Company. But he wanted to use his camera to tell a different story.

He submitted an idea for a photo essay on the leader of a Harlem gang to *Life*

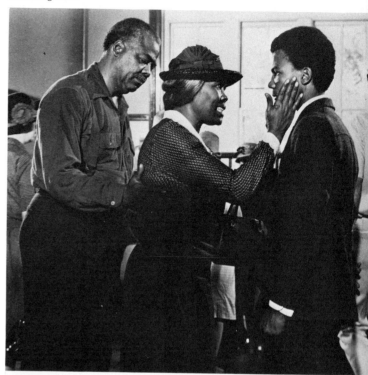

magazine in 1958. It was accepted. Weeks afterward, Parks was on his way to Paris to cover the fashion openings for *Life.* He stayed on in Paris as a *Life* staffer. "In Paris," he wrote, "I was able to concentrate. I began to compose music, write poetry, and to think of writing about my childhood." While working for *Life* he reported on segregation in the South, crime, the Black Muslims, Mohammed Ali, and Stokely Carmichael. One of his finest photo essays was the story of Flavio, a boy from a Brazilian ghetto who took care of six younger brothers and sisters, though he was afflicted with asthma and tuberculosis and was suffering from malnutrition. After Flavio's story appeared in *Life,* Parks returned to Brazil with motion picture equipment. The result was his first film. His other short films were *The World of Piri Thomas* and *The Diary of a Harlem Family.*

Gordon Parks has written volumes of poetry, fiction, autobiography. His concertos and symphonies have been performed by orchestras in New York, Philadelphia and Venice. In 1968 he went home to Fort Scott to film *The Learning Tree* and became the first black director of a major-studio, big-money film. "A questionable honor," Parks says. But the film was a great success. Then in 1971, less than a month after Van Peebles' *Sweet Sweetback's Baadasssss Song,* Gordon Parks' second film, *Shaft,* opened in downtown Manhattan. Parks likes to quote critic Maurice Peterson, who described *Shaft* as "the first picture to show a black man who leads a life free of racial torment." A year later, *Shaft's Big Score* appeared, followed by *Shaft in Africa.* At least two more sequels are planned.

Richard Roundtree in Shaft (1971)

Melvin
Van Peebles

Melvin Van Peebles was born on the south side of Chicago in 1932; his father was a tailor. Van is his middle name. After graduating from Ohio Wesleyan in 1953 he joined the air force and served for three years as navigator on a B-47. He spent a brief time in Mexico painting, then moved to San Francisco where he worked as a grip on a cable car. He was fired. He then tried working at the post office. He was fired.

During that time he made a few short films, and with hopes that they would open studio doors to him he went to Hollywood. He got two job offers—one to run an elevator, the other to work as a parking lot attendant. He decided to move to Holland to study astronomy. There he began to work with the Dutch National Theatre and toured with them in Brendan Behan's play *The Hostage*. A representative of the French Cinematheque who had seen his short films invited him to come to Paris. Van Peebles hitched a ride and arrived broke but eager to work. As he later described it: "they said 'it's great you could come.' That's all. No job. No money . . . . I kept getting thrown in jail for begging. I didn't have a beggar's card. I used to dance in the streets and sing 'Ole Man River.' I thought, Jesus Christ, is that what I came here for?"

He discovered that French filmmaking was as closed an industry as American filmmaking—but there was one loophole. In France an author who wants to film his own work is granted a government subsidy and a director's card. Van Peebles taught himself French and began to write. His first two novels were written in English, then translated. The third was written directly in French. He published five in all and one of them, *La Permis-*

sion, became *The Story of a Three-Day Pass*. He filmed it in 1967 and it became the French entry in the San Francisco film festival.

The day he walked into the film festival offices, a secretary looked at him and said, "Over there."

"Over where?" he asked.

"Over there. Weren't you sent to fix the lights?"

"I'm the French delgate," he replied, and later said, "It was a kick. Nobody believed it."

On the strength of *Three-Day Pass* he signed a contract with Columbia to make *Watermelon Man* (1970). He then used the $70,000 he earned from *Watermelon*, and money borrowed from various other sources, to finance *Sweet Sweetback's Baadasssss Song* (1971), which he produced, directed, starred in, edited, and scored. And practically single-handedly he found an audience for it. Ignoring the critic's reaction, he went directly to what he calls "his constituency"—on the street. "This movie is black life, unpandered. If the critics want to see it, let them go to a theatre that's full of black people and full of kids and let them lis-

ten to what's coming down and they'll understand the film." It has since become the all-time top independent money-maker.

Using the material from his record albums, Van Peebles next put together *Ain't Supposed to Die a Natural Death*, a collection of songs, dances, and narrations to music. It opened on Broadway in October of 1971. With the help of Ossie Davis, Van Peebles promoted the show to the street people he had written it for. When it was finally established, he began working on *Don't Play Us Cheap*, an adaptation of one of his novels. In his typically unorthodox way, he first filmed on location in New Mexico, then brought the play to Broadway, where it opened in May of 1972. The film version is scheduled to be released in the fall of 1973. Van Peebles premiered his next work, *Out There by Your Lonesome*—"an evening of singing, rapping, and running it down"—at Riker's Island prison, saying, "Some folks tour colleges. But most of my constituency is right here."

Since 1967 Van Peebles has earned millions of dollars. He says, "I'm not in-

to the business for the money. I'm into the money for the business." The name of his corporation is Yeah, Inc. He was one of the first to speak of "the black esthetic" in films: "I want white people to approach *Sweetback* the way they do an Italian or Japanese film. They have to understand *our* culture . . . . I don't need moral victories. I got them up to here. Like in *The Alamo*, the black slave is freed and he says, 'I'se free, boss. I suppose I'll stay heah wid you on de farm.' That doesn't go down any more . . . . You keep the moral victories. But let me win."

Around Melvin Van Peebles' neck is a tatooed necklace with the words "cut on the dotted line" inscribed beside it in French. And on his buttock in a West African warrior language—"if you can."

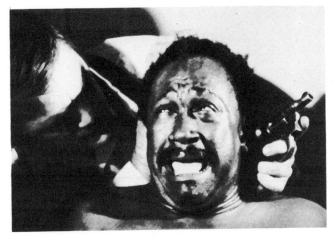

Richard Roundtree

"Shaft's his name and Shaft's his game." And according to his current contract, Richard Roundtree will be Shaft at least seven times. Relatively unknown before *Shaft*, Roundtree was the first black actor to be given a careful, conscientious, star build-up. His wardrobe—leather jackets and knit turtlenecks—was selected with the greatest care, a barber was on hand to attend to his hair style, and two days were spent with make-up men building the perfect moustache on his upper lip. He spent hours working out in a gym and more hours in target practice and in learning how to handle the weapons he used in the film. And there were endless rehearsal hours in which he practiced striding across busy Manhattan streets without looking—in order to create the impression that John Shaft, superhero, owned the place.

With the release of *Shaft*, Roundtree was at once compared to Bogart, Cagney, and Edward G. Robinson. The film, which was packaged and promoted for a black audience, grossed $6 million in the first two months after its premiere. Its critics called it "second-string Mickey Spillane" and a "B-grade gutpuncher." Some blacks asked, "Do we really have

Richard Roundtree as John Shaft

time for a Shaft?" and critic Clayton Riley described it as a "Hip Black Movie which doesn't have to deal in any real fashion with what Black life is actually all about." But Riley added: "Of course American films have never had to deal with anything real and certainly shouldn't be expected to start now."

At any rate, *Shaft* and its sequels, *Shaft's Big Score* and *Shaft in Africa*, have made Richard Roundtree, whose friends call him "Tree," a star.

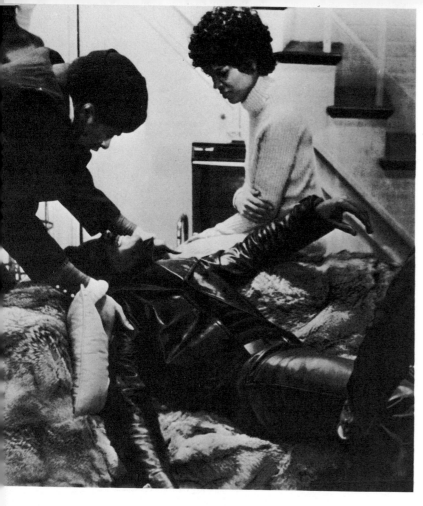

Roundtree was born in New Rochelle, New York, where his mother worked as a housekeeper and his father as chauffeur, garbage man, and elder of the local Pentacostal Church, where he preached every third Sunday. He remembers a warm, comfortable childhood. Of his years at New Rochelle High School, he told an interviewer: "Football brought me something when I started playing in high school. I was good for something for more people than just my family. All you have to do is hear all that handclapping. You're addicted!"

New Rochelle was the nation's third-ranking high school football team and Roundtree was its star end. He was also captain of the track team and voted most popular, best dressed, and best looking in his senior class. And he won a football scholarship to Southern Illinois University. But he tired of the Saturday afternoon pummeling and his interests turned instead to the drama workshop—where "all the pretty girls hung out."

By the middle of his sophomore year he had decided to drop out. He returned to New York and worked as a janitor at New Rochelle City Hall, then as a salesman at Barney's men's clothing store. Then he tried modeling: "That was just when they decided to use black models because they realized we shaved and drank beer just like other human beings." This was a success. When he first met Muhammed Ali, Ali greeted him by asking, "Hey, ain't you the cat on the Duke Hair Spray can?"

Through all of this he had been toying with the idea of studying acting seriously. Encouraged by friends, such as Bill Cosby, for one, he joined the Negro Ensemble Company in 1967 and soon got roles in *Man, Better Man, Kongi's Harvest*, and then the lead in *Mau Mau Room*. His first screen appearance was a one-minute bit in *What Do You Say to a Naked Lady?* He was playing the lead in the Philadelphia road company production of *The Great White Hope* when he was called to audition for the part of John Shaft.

In a recent interview in *Life* magazine, Roundtree talked about a plantation he had seen while driving through Virgina. The big house and some of the original slave cabins were still standing. "You know what I'd like to do?" he asked. "I'd like to buy that place and turn it over to my grandmother. She's 103 and she's fantastic. I think she should have that place. That would just about wrap it all up, wouldn't it?"

Ron O'Neal

Ron O'Neal in scenes from Super Fly (1972)

In 1970, Ron O'Neal had a hard decision to make. After having been in the theatre for twelve years with no great success, he was offered a part in an off-Broadway production at a salary of $100 a week. At the same time, he was offered the lead in Charles Gordone's *No Place to be Somebody* at New York's Public Theatre with no salary. O'Neal chose *No Place to be Somebody* because it was the role he had been waiting for; the play was a smash hit, moved to Broadway, and O'Neal won four major awards for his performance.

He was born in 1937 in the Cleveland ghetto. His father, once a jazz musician who had played with Jelly Roll Morton and in *Blackbirds of 1929* had turned to factory work to support his family. After high school O'Neal entered Ohio State University but flunked out after a semester and returned to Cleveland. Aimless, wandering, looking for something to do, he was taken by a friend to see *Finian's Rainbow* at Cleveland's interracial Karamu Theater. O'Neal joined the theatre company and remained with them for eight years, playing everything from Walter Younger in *A Raisin in the Sun* to Stanley Kowalski in *A Streetcar Named Desire*.

In 1964 he came to New York, where he worked for a Haryou Act program, teaching acting and performing with his troupe in jails, schools, and settlement houses. Then he worked as part of a touring company, played in *Show Boat* in summer stock, and finally won his Equity card.

After *No Place To Be Somebody* closed, O'Neal had his awards to comfort him, but no work to speak of. He

played a few small parts on television and appeared in the Sidney Poitier film, *The Organization,* and the Negro Ensemble Company's production of *Dream.* Light-skinned, with long straight hair, O'Neal feels his looks prevented him from getting many parts during that period. "I don't fit into any of the myths," he told an interviewer.

Finally, a friend asked him to collaborate on a film treatment which, if produced, would have a starring role for him. He agreed, and the film became *Super Fly* (1972). As Priest, the movie's pusher-hero, O'Neal created his own myth. And as both star and director of *Super Fly T.N.T.* (1973), filmed both in Africa and Europe, O'Neal is now able to say with confidence, "I want to go where the power is, where the money is, where the control is."

Diana Ross

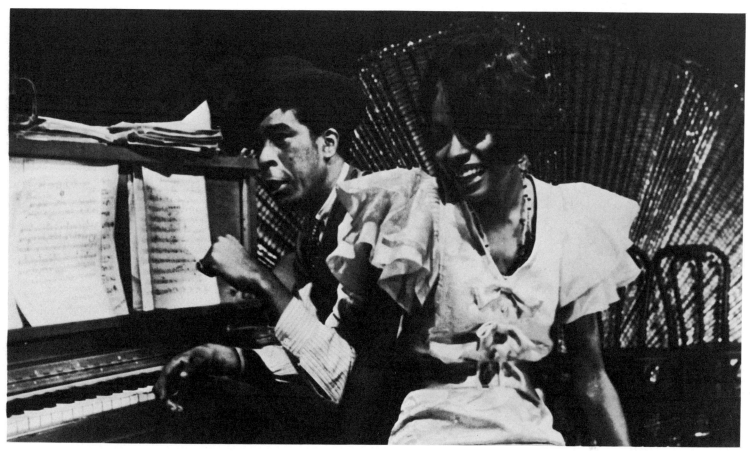

Richard Pryor, as Piano Man, befriends the young Billie Holiday at her first audition, in Lady Sings the Blues *(1972).*

When she was fourteen years old Diana Ross, together with Mary Wilson and Florence Ballard, walked into the offices of the newly formed Motown Records in Detroit and asked for an audition, calling themselves the "Primettes." The three had been singing together since they met in a local Baptist church choir.

"Motown," Ross said, "turned me away and told me to go back to school." She did, meanwhile working at an after-school job as a busgirl in the cafeteria of Hudson's department store, and designing and sewing costumes for the trio, which continued to practice and sing at small jobs around the city. She is the second eldest of six children, who all grew up in a housing project in a poor section of Detroit. Her father worked for a brass manufacturing company and later became the foreman. A self-described tomboy, Diana Ross remembers with pleasure the foot races she invariably won at the company's summer picnics. Though the family had little money she recalled the period as a happy one: "There was always a nickel to get a candy bar. I never felt terribly deprived because we had a little bit of everything. We were happy kids and sang

Lady sings the blues, by now using drugs to keep her going.

hymns in church and rock-and-roll on street corners."

Her childhood and later life held none of the horrors that shaped the life of Billie Holiday, whose film biography was to make her a movie star and Academy Award nominee in 1972.

After she graduated from high school, the group went back to Motown. Finally they were allowed to make a demo. They were singing "There Goes My Baby" when Berry Gordy, Motown's young president, walked in. He listened and enrolled them in his "artist's development" course. "Then we started to work," Diana Ross explained. "We learned how to sit, how to walk . . . even how to hold a cigarette." And how to polish a perfor-

mance. As the "Supremes," they became the smoothest and most professional exponents of the Motown pop-shouting sound.

After recording a few singles, they hit the top of the charts with "Where Did Our Love Go?" The hits that followed included "Baby Love" and "Stop in the Name of Love." During the next ten years of constant touring, the Supremes, with their high, smooth hair-dos, huge velvety eyes, and blazing sequined gowns, sold over twenty-five million records. By the time she had reached her mid-twenties, Diana Ross was a millionaire. She remembers those years as one long bus ride interrupted by one-night stands. The group was as heavily chaperoned as a trio of Spanish princesses.

Motown president Berry Gordy, who financed *Lady Sings the Blues*, has remained Diana Ross' principal advisor and good friend since the beginning of her career. In 1969 she decided to leave the Supremes. In her first solo appearance on a Dinah Shore NBC television special she wore feathers, spangles, and snakey body paint and sang a torrid version of "Aquarius" from the rock musical *Hair*. She recorded solo for a while, and then came *Lady Sings the Blues* (1972). From its inception the film was planned as a vehicle for Diana Ross. She studied Billie Holiday's life, talked to many of her friends and fellow musicians, and for nine months before filming began, listened to her records for hours every day.

"Diana Ross is Billie Holiday," the movie ads said. Those who knew Billie Holiday disagree. The film was in many ways unfaithful to the facts of Lady Day's life. Reviews were mixed. But the reviewers were unanimous in their praise of Diana Ross' performance, calling her an astonishingly fine actress. Critic Pauline Kael wrote: "Diana Ross, a tall skinny goblin of a girl, intensely likeable, always in motion, seemed an irrational choice for the sultry, still Billie Holiday, yet she's like a beautiful bonfire: there's nothing to question—you just react with everything you've got .... She's ... striking and special—an original."

Billie Dee Williams as Louis McKay confronts Lady Day after the show.

Cicely Tyson

Tyson with Sammy Davis in A Man Called Adam

"I was working as a secretary," Cicely Tyson recalled in a recent interview. "And one day I sat there banging away at the typewriter for the American Red Cross and I was suddenly overwhelmed by this mechanical routine thing I was doing. I pushed myself away from the desk and said to myself that I knew God didn't put me here on this earth to bang on a typewriter for the rest of my life. There had to be something else for me to do." She went out looking for something else. At first, it was modeling: she became one of the ten top black models in the country, earning sixty-five dollars an hour. Later, after she had read for a part in an independent film, it was acting. Though the film was never made, she was hooked.

Her first break came, as did Calvin Lockhart's, in the Harlem production of *Dark of the Moon*. She went from there to the famous off-Broadway production of *The Blacks*. For her performance in *Moon on a Rainbow Shawl* in 1962, she won that year's Vernon Rice Award.

In 1963, she was featured with George C. Scott on the television series, *East Side, West Side.*

Cicely Tyson grew up in Harlem, where her parents had moved from Nevis, the smallest of the Leeward Islands in the Caribbean. She says, "I grew up on welfare. My father had a pushcart and my mother did a day's work now and again as a domestic." But for Cicely and her brother and sister, there were almost always hot meals left on the radiator to stay warm when her mother went out to work. Her parents separated when she was eleven, and Cicely sold shopping bags on the street to earn money. Even then, she knew there was "something outside the ghetto. I would jump on a bus or a train, ride to the end and get out and look around...." When she graduated from Charles Evans Hughes High School, she went to work as a typist for the Red Cross—until she had had enough of typing!

As a child, she remembers the family's social life centering around the church. "I was brought up in a religious atmosphere. I sang in the choir in the mornings, there were prayer meetings on Wednesdays, choir rehearsals on Fridays and then, of course, in addition to attending Sunday services, I played the piano in Sunday School. Most of the social functions I attended were given by the church, St. John's Episcopal in lower Harlem. 'My mother still goes there." Cicely was never allowed to go to the movies. When later, her mother heard she planned to become an actress, she refused to speak to her.

During the sixties, Cicely Tyson appeared in *The Comedians* (1967), *A Man Called Adam* (1966), and *The Heart Is a Lonely Hunter* (1968). After that, she turned down role after role, rejecting the sterotype of prostitute, junkie, or

Tyson with Alan Arkin in The Heart is a Lonely Hunter

maid. Finally, in 1972 came *Sounder* and stardom. And an Academy Award nomination. Tyson says of her role in *Sounder:* "Rebecca is the first positive portrayal of a black woman on the screen. Always before she has been a con woman, a prostitute, a drug addict. The time has come for blacks to look back at our history and be proud of it and not ashamed."

Sounder was screened at the Atlanta Film Festival in the summer of 1972. Cicely Tyson was there and the audience gave her a five minute standing ovation. Later, she was named Best Actress. She said of that occasion, "All I could say to myself was, 'This is Atlanta, Georgia and here I am.'"

Tyson with Paul Winfield, Yvonne Harrell, Eric Hooks, Kevin Hooks, and Taj Mahal in Sounder

Ten years after the march on Washington, one hundred ten years after the Emancipation Proclamation, we look back. From *Sambo* to *The Birth of a Nation* to *The Green Pastures* to *Stormy Weather* to *Porgy and Bess* to *Shaft*. And so we stand. Perhaps one day they'll make a movie about Bert Williams or Paul Robeson or Juano Hernandez that will tell the real story of blacks in films. But meanwhile, it is only for us to wonder how far along the road we really have come.

Al Young, poet, novelist, and teacher, says in *New Black Voices*: "There is now taking place a heady flowering of black genius unlike anything that's been experienced before.

"This whole business of art as hustle—which seems to be where we've come to at this stage of the interminable 20th Century—has to be challenged. I've always believed the individual human heart to be more revolutionary than any political party or platform."

Bibliography

Allen, Frederick L. *Big Change: America Transforms Itself.* New York: Harper & Row, 1952.

American Film Institute. *The American Film Institute Catalogue: Feature Films 1921-30.* Vol. 2. New York: R.R. Bowker, 1971.

Bowen, David. *The Struggle Within: Race Relations in The United States.* New York: Grosset & Dunlap, 1972.

Brownlow, Kevin. *The Parade's Gone By* . . . . New York: Knopf, 1968.

Chapman, Abraham, ed. *New Black Voices.* New York: New American Library, 1972.

Charters, Ann. *Nobody: The Story of Bert Williams.* New York: Macmillan Co., 1970.

Davis, Sammy, Jr. *Yes, I Can.* Edited by Jane and Burt Boyar. New York: Farrar, Straus & Giroux, 1965.

Drotning, P. *A Guide to Negro History in America.* Garden City, N.Y.: Doubleday, 1968.

DuBois, W.E.B. *Souls of Black Folks.* 1903. Reprint. New York: Johnson Reprints, 1969.

Fletcher, Tom. *100 Years of the Negro in Show Business: The Tom Fletcher Story.* New York: Burdge, 1954.

Gertner, Richard, ed. *1973 International Motion Picture Almanac.* New York: Quigley, 1973.

Griffith, Richard. *The Movie Stars.* Garden City, N.Y.: Doubleday, 1970.

Hoffman, William. *Sidney.* New York: Lyle Stuart, 1971.

Horne, Lena and Schickel, Richard. *Lena.* Garden City, N.Y.: Doubleday, 1965.

Hornsby, Alton, Jr. *The Black Almanac.* Woodbury, N.Y.: Barron's Educational Series, 1972.

Hoyt, Edwin P. *Paul Robeson: The American Othello,* Cleveland: World, 1967.

Hughes, Langston and Meltzer, Milton. *A Pictorial History of the Negro in America.* New York: Crown, 1963

_____.*Black Magic; a Pictorial History of the Negro in American Entertainment.* Englewood Cliffs, N.J.: Prentice-Hall, 1967.

Jerome, Victor J. *The Negro in Hollywood Films.* New York: Masses & Mainstream, 1950.

Katz, William. *Eyewitness: The Negro in American History.* New York: Pitman, 1967.

Lomax, Louis E. *The Negro Revolt.* New York: Harper & Row, 1962.

Malcolm X. *Autobiography of Malcolm X.* Edited by Alex Haley. New York: Grove Press, 1965.

Mapp, Edward. *Blacks in American Films: Today and Yesterday.* Metuchen, N.J.: Scarecrow Press, 1972.

The New York Times Directory of the Film. New York: Arno/Random House, 1971.

Noble, Peter. *The Negro in Films.* 1949. Reprint. New York: Arno, 1970.

Parks, Gordon. *A Choice of Weapons.* New York: Harper & Row, 1965.

Patterson, Lindsay, comp. *Anthology of the American Negro in the Theatre.* New York: United Publishers, 1970.

Ploski, Harry A. and Brown, Roscoe C., eds. *The Negro Almanac.* New York: Bellwether, 1962.

Robeson, Paul. *Here I Stand.* Boston: Beacon Press, 1971.

Schuster, Mel, comp. *Motion Picture Performers: A Bibliography of Magazine and Periodical Articles 1900-1969.* Metuchen, N.J.: Scarecrow Press, 1971.

Shaw, Arnold. *Belafonte, An Unauthorized Biography.* Philadelphia: Chilton, 1960.

Time-Life Books. *This Fabulous Century.* 7 vols. New York: Time-Life Books, 1970.

Waters, Ethel and Samuels, Charles. *His Eye Is on the Sparrow.* Garden City, N.Y.: Doubleday, 1951.

Index